C

FIELD
OF
MYSTE⅃

The Crop Circle Phenomenon in Sussex

Andy Thomas

S.B. Publications

To Kaye, for her (almost) unending patience

First published in 1996 by S.B. Publications
c/o 19 Grove Road, Seaford, East Sussex, BN25 1TP

Reprinted 1996

ISBN 1 85770 096 1

Typeset and printed by Island Press Ltd.
Tel: 01323 490222 UK

CONTENTS

Front & Back Cover: Crop formations at East Dean, near Chichester, 1994. *Photo: Steve Alexander.*

Title Page: Spectacular roadside view of the complex of formations at Cissbury Ring, 1995. *Photo: Andy Thomas.*

ACKNOWLEDGEMENTS

No reference book is truly the work of one person and some of the information included throughout has been gathered from a variety of sources. Whilst it is impossible to list all deserving souls, particular acknowledgement must go to the following, in alphabetical order, all of whom have contributed significantly to crop circle research in Sussex and beyond:

Steve Alexander, Marcus Allen, Charles Besly, Kim Besly, Di Brown, Peggy Bunt, Paul Bura, John Cole, Carole Coren, Adam Cotton, Karen Douglas, Griller Gilgannon, Larry Grant, Michael Green, Will Harris, Terry Harrison, John Holloway, Michael Hubbard, Nick James, John Martineau, Judith Newman, Martin Noakes, Debbie Pardoe, Keith Parker, Jason Porthouse, Mark Porthouse, Diana Pratt, Ted Richards, David Tait, Nigel Tomsett and *Karen Wolf* with apologies to anyone inadvertently missed out.

Credit must be given for the important scientific work carried out on plant samples from many Sussex crop formations by *Nancy Talbott, Dr W C Levengood* and *John Burke* of the BLT Research team at the Pinelandia Biophysical and Am-Tech laboratories in the USA.

Special mention must also go to all the farmers who have helped crop circle researchers over the years and enabled work to be carried out on their land. Their co-operation is much appreciated.

Huge thanks must be expressed to everyone who helped directly in the compiling of this book (some of whom also belong in the lists above) and especially to those who donated photographs from their archives, all credited in the captions.

Special thanks to the following:

Tom Fenn, Roger and *Marion Fenn, John Eccles* of the *Sussex Express, Peter* and *Veronica Lenihan, Pat Stancombe, Brian Emmett, Nigel Tomsett, Carole Cochrane, Jenni Cassel* and *Mary Bennett.*

Extreme gratitude to the following:

The Right Hon Lord Healey for his time, photographs and preface.

Michael Glickman for his charming foreword.

David and *Anne Tilt* for their hospitality and vital information on early formations.

David Russell for his hospitality, complete access to all personal archives and for drafting the maps.

Steve Benz for providing the spark for this book.

And, most importantly...

Barry Reynolds for checking facts, making helpful suggestions, providing archive material, map references, and much more.

Kaye Thomas for proof-reading, advice and more besides.

Thank you everyone.

PREFACE

BY THE RIGHT HON LORD HEALEY OF RIDDLESDEN

On Saturday morning 28th July 1984, I went, as usual, shopping in Seaford. On the way back to Alfriston, as I crossed the top of High and Over, my attention was distracted from the wonderful view of the Cuckmere valley by a sight I have never forgotten and still do not understand.

In the middle of the cornfield below there was a perfect circle some forty feet across which seemed to have been pressed into the corn by some unknown agency. There were also four smaller circles of exactly the same radius from the centre of the large one at right angles to each other.

I rushed home for my camera to photograph the scene. Later the *Daily Mail* just beat the *Daily Mirror* in the competition to print my photographs. A careful study of my prints offered no hint of what or who was responsible for making the circles although a wavering path through the corn to the larger circle showed that someone, or something, had entered the site.

At the time I had no idea that there had been a few similar crop circles in Sussex in earlier years. I could not guess that the phenomenon would be repeated many times in the following decade - mainly on the chalk downs in southern England, but also in other parts of Britain and the world.

Since that sighting I have read many articles and books about crop circles. There is no doubt that in recent years some have been created by hoaxers. However, I was impressed by an article from my friend and colleague Lord Solly Zuckerman, one of the leading scientists of this century, reviewing some of this material for the *New York Review of Books*. He had to admit that, as with extra-sensory perception and UFOs, there is a residue of cases for which so far no explanation has been offered which is compatible with the world as we know it through science.

Andy Thomas' book records the incidence of crop circles in Sussex over the last two decades. It is a valuable addition to the history of one of the mysteries of our time.

DENIS HEALEY

Standing inside a glorious crop formation in oilseed rape, Southease, 1995 (95/01). Photo: Andy Thomas

FOREWORD

Some years ago I spent a weekend with John Martineau and his family on the Welsh borders. For those not familiar with that name, John is a young crop circle researcher who has produced a geometrical analysis of the circles which, for many, remains the zenith of crop circle research.

On the first night, I found that John had thoughtfully provided bedtime reading. A small pile of *Sussex Circulars* was on the bedside table. Certainly, I had heard rumours about this little magazine but had never read it. I stayed awake for hours and was bleary-eyed at breakfast.

What started as a monthly information sheet for Sussex crop circle enthusiasts, edited by Andy Thomas, has now grown (via an enigmatic name-change to SC) to become the best-informed and most widely read crop circle publication. For anyone interested in this most beautiful of phenomena, SC has become, in a small number of years, required reading.

Let me now admit a personal interest. Some time ago, I was invited to write a regular column for SC, an invitation I accepted with unseemly glee and haste. I am proud to be part of the team (and by a sort of osmosis, an honorary 'Sussex Boy') and delighted to be working with an editor of the calibre of Andy Thomas. He brings to SC, as he brings to this book, a very particular ability.

The crop circle question, like other areas on the fringes of knowledge, produces extremes of position. Many, when confronted with these astonishments, discover reserves of conservatism, even denial, within themselves. Others excitedly pursue fringe notions which, even to a crackpot like myself, are simply lunatic.

Andy Thomas' great strength, as both editor and author, is his ability to bring a sober discernment to all aspects of the crop circle phenomenon without ever dismissing any possibility or prejudging any circumstance. This requires a rare maturity and nerve.

This book is informed by the same care and openness and takes a position which, I believe, is unique in the history of the subject.

Imagine the intellectual chaos which has occurred here. Circles have been appearing for fifteen, twenty or is it two hundred years? No-one knows. Have there been three, five or six thousand events? We are not sure. They appear in eight, twelve or over twenty countries. Or do they? And these are the sort of conundrums which arise before we even start to consider the nature of the circle itself.

What a delight, then, to have a book which for the first time, is limited and precise in its intention. Though fully aware of the scale of this mystery, Andy Thomas limits the study, at least geographically, to Sussex and the events that have occurred there.

The neatness of this approach brings real delights. Andy Thomas is in a perfect position to write the book and he does so with thoroughness. Every crop circle known to have appeared in Sussex during the last few years is listed, it is described in as much detail as is available and the relevant story of its discovery and examination is told. The bigger issues are never very far away and, even in an examination of this limited canvas, one is aware of the larger mysteries and the more fundamental questions yet to be answered.

This is an essential component of the library of every crop circle researcher and a perfect introduction to this wonderful enigma.

MICHAEL GLICKMAN

Writer and inventor Michael Glickman is one of the most prominent and respected researchers on the crop circle phenomenon.

Circle surveying tools at the centre of the 1995 Cissbury Ring Formation (95/10). Photo: Andy Thomas

INTRODUCTION

The media ridicules them. Eminent scientists dismiss them. Yet crop circles, those enigmatic and elaborate shapes found in meadows each summer continue to appear, their origin and purpose a complete mystery. Two of the major sites for the crop circle phenomenon are the counties of East and West Sussex on the south-east coast of England, which have seen several decades of ongoing circle activity...

In that magical moment as my first sighting of a crop formation came distantly into view through the rising morning mist while honeymooning in Wiltshire in 1991, I somehow knew that my life would never be the same again. I wasn't wrong. I didn't know what had caused this incredible symbol to appear in the field before me, I only knew that here was a phenomenon that I had to get closer to, to understand, to simply be part of in some way. I learnt after, that my experience was not unique; many others had been affected in the same way.

When I returned to my home county of East Sussex, I learnt from a friend that he had seen a crop circle here too, at Poynings, near Devil's Dyke. I was astonished; these intriguing mysteries were here on my own doorstep! My investigations led me to become a member of the Centre for Crop Circle Studies (CCCS) and through this organisation I became involved with others in setting up a Sussex-based team of dedicated circle-hunters, recording and researching crop formations as they appeared. Throughout this work we have had many incredible experiences, and gained insights which would have eluded us without the presence of the circles in our lives, whatever may be behind them.

This book is the story of the many crop formations which have appeared in East and West Sussex in the last few decades, a guidebook and a fascinating journey of discovery through the ancient vistas of these beautiful counties, revealing a mysterious landscape where strange and seemingly magical events occur on a regular basis, events which sceptics are still at a loss to explain, despite their continued efforts. Sussex provides an excellent macrocosm of the circle phenomenon as a whole, which is now global; examining the events which have occurred here puts the crop circles under a magnifying glass, recording important details rarely discussed elsewhere.

It does not, however, attempt to provide a solution to the crop circle mystery. No-one has, as yet, found an answer that successfully pieces together all the many parts of this strange puzzle. What it may perhaps achieve, if you are new to this phenomenon, is to make you ask your own questions about the extraordinary events occurring in the fields around us and their significance, if any. Most of all it may inspire you to question severely what you have been told about crop circles in the media by those who would rather we did nothing but laugh at things that are not understood, jumping on easy and mundane answers instead of looking at the facts. Even if the enquiries this book inspires are simply those you started with, you will at least be able to make them on a more informed basis!

Regardless of what might be behind these incredible appearing shapes, one thing is clear; the crop circles have changed many people's lives. The seemingly multi-cultural symbols touch the hearts of those who encounter them in ways which are hard to define yet are tangible in the transformation of personalities, usually for the better, and expanding outlooks. The questions raised by the unexplained presence of these wonders invariably lead to greater contemplation of the true nature of the world and the surrounding universe. Whatever their real purpose, no-one can deny that the crop formations are acting as catalysts for spiritual growth and, by implication, world change.

The information throughout this book has been collected together from my own research and the work of others (see acknowledgements) into the crop circle phenomenon in Sussex. As interest in the circles has grown over a period of time, so it follows that the information and stories collected in recent years is far more comprehensive than that of earlier ones, thus the later chapters are the more detailed and involved.

Throughout the book, I refer to the source responsible for the crop circles as "the circle-making force", in the absence of any firmer understanding or description which can be applied. No connotation suggesting a source of any particular nature is attached to this, although research does seem to suggest that some kind of 'energy', possibly microwave, is involved in the process of laying down the crop inside circles, but even that cannot be certain. What triggers that process is a question that still remains.

While this book is as informative as possible, it does not exist as a technical manual, and as such, the given dimensions of formations are kept to a minimum. In most cases, where the measurements are known, only a few sample dimensions are recorded to give the reader an understanding of the scale involved (usually the size of the major circles, or total lengths of formations). These figures are given to the nearest imperial foot. Circle sizes are always given as diameters. Most crop 'circles' are not perfectly circular but elliptical, and measurements can vary depending on where across the circle they were taken. Here, the largest figures recorded are given. The silhouette diagrams are not to be taken as precise surveys but are purely a pictorial reference and are not shown to scale with each other. Extensive and exact measurements for most crop formations since 1992 are held by CCCS Sussex and have been published in *SC* magazine (see appendices), for which back issues are available.

Specific dates for the arrival of crop formations are sometimes hard to pin down if their appearance is not recorded immediately, in the sure knowledge that the field was empty the previous day. Where exact information is not available, dates have been approximated as accurately as possible.

Similarly, exact map references for crop formations are often only known if their position has been recorded as part of the official on-the-spot survey (this is generally the case for post-1991 events). Where this information isn't known, map references have been approximated from the study of photographs and anecdotal evidence. In extreme cases (especially the early formations) where almost nothing is known, the map reference given is simply that of the nearest named town or village to a reported sighting. Out of respect for farmers' privacy, the names of the farms which own the land where formations appear have been omitted. Throughout the book, it is assumed that all the events being discussed, unless otherwise denoted, are in Sussex. Although East and West Sussex are two separate counties, the two are treated as one here, as in Centre for Crop Circle Studies investigations, and no differentiation is made in the text. The exact locations, which *do* give this information, with map references, can be found on the charts which begin each chapter, and in the maps provided in the appendices.

For each formation recorded in Sussex there is a reference number which is used universally by CCCS Sussex and these are denoted in brackets within the text so that they can be referred to on the charts. The reference numbers are usually made up from the year, followed by the sequential number of the formation that year, ie. '94/03', although occasionally (especially in earlier years) these numbers do not follow chronologically if some numbers were allocated before the knowledge of other earlier formations came to light.

It has been impossible to include photographs of every pattern (in some cases good photographic material doesn't exist). Pictures have thus been chosen for their aesthetic qualities or points of interest. Incidentally, ragged pathways which cross the fields, visible in some photographs, are simply where visitors have entered the fields to look at the designs without walking up the tractor 'tramlines' and are not parts of the formations themselves or evidence of hoaxers!

Lastly, the information in this book is as comprehensive as possible given the limitations of the format, and inevitably some fine details (such as findings made through dowsing, mathematical geometry work, etc.) are referred to only briefly, as it is difficult to do justice to such subjects with brevity. Much of this type of investigation has been published more fully elsewhere, notably in SC magazine. All the formations listed in the book are those that investigation has unearthed so far. It may be that some readers, alerted to the subject, will know of others in Sussex that have been missed here. If so, we at CCCS Sussex would like to hear from you! An address is given in the appendices.

ANDY THOMAS

The farmer surveys the new arrival on his land at Felbridge, East Grinstead, in 1993 (93/08). Photo: C. Emmett

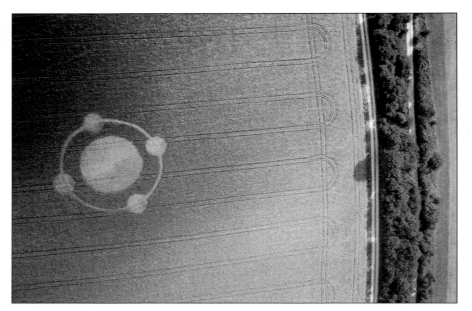

Second of two celtic cross formations at Sompting in 1993 (93/05). This later grew an extra 'grapeshot' circle. Photo: Michael Hubbard.

Inside the vast Cissbury Ring formation of 1995 (95/10). Photo: Steve Alexander

THE CROP CIRCLE PHENOMENON:
AN OVERALL VIEW

Before delving into the rich history of crop formations in Sussex, a general overview and understanding of the entire crop circle phenomenon is necessary to see how local events fit into a far wider picture. This chapter seeks to provide a brief - and by the nature of something brief, far from definitive - explanation and history of what exactly crop circles are and how they have developed into one of the most exciting mysteries of modern times.

What Is A Crop Circle?

Crop circles are patterns found mysteriously pressed into crop fields in the summer months. These patterns are also known as corn circles, crop formations or agriglyphs, a term reserved for the more elaborate designs. Usually circular (as their name suggests) in the basic components which make up the designs, more often than not they also embody other shapes in various combinations. No crop seems immune to the phenomenon and formations are regularly found in wheat, barley, oats, rye, oilseed rape and occasionally less common ones, such as maize. Circles have also been found in wild uncultivated areas of grass and undergrowth, in water-logged paddy-fields, sand, snow and even in ice on frozen rivers.

The plants inside a crop circle are usually laid down and swirled in a very neat spiral, either clockwise or anticlockwise - sometimes both. Also found have been radial lays splayed out from the centre, S-shape swirls, multi-directional flows and, more controversially, even crop simply bent over halfway up the stems. No mechanical or

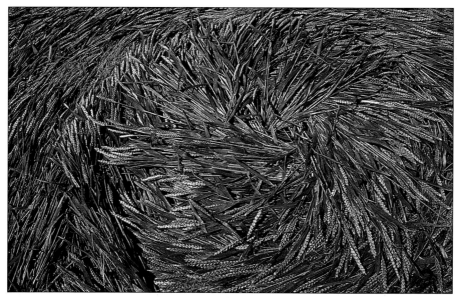

Centre of a formation at Patcham, 1992 (92/04) showing the intricate and beautiful swirled effects often found. Photo: Andy Thomas

Patcham, 1992 (92/04) showing how pathways often spill gorgeously into connecting circles.
Photo: Andy Thomas.

physical pressure seems to have been applied to the plants in most cases, the stems remaining completely undamaged. Once laid down in a crop formation, the plants continue to ripen as normal, although research like that of Dr W C Levengood of the Pinelandia Biophysical Laboratories in the US is showing that subtle changes take place inside circle-affected crop. This involves the elongation of nodal joints and microscopic damage to the cell walls inside, suggesting that a very brief but intense heat has been applied, possibly microwave in origin. Other effects such as bending at the nodal joints, enabling stems to sweep around corners and achieve particular shapes, have also been observed (impossible to replicate by hand without breaking the plant - this bending is not to be confused with phototropism where stalks, when flattened, grow naturally back towards the light from the nodes).

Crop formations appear in all types of size and shape, some small and simple, others huge and complex. In the majority of cases they appear overnight, undetected until the following morning when they are excitedly discovered and reported, although there are reports of ones appearing in daylight. There are a number of eye-witness reports of crop patterns being laid down by an invisible force in a matter of seconds. Many sightings have been documented of unusual lights and luminosities appearing in the sky above sites where circles are subsequently discovered. Strange lights have also been witnessed, and filmed, moving about inside existing formations. No non-human-made crop formation has yet been filmed being created, despite many attempts, although there are rumours that such footage exists. One infamous experiment in 1991, using infra-red cameras and motion-detectors around an enclosed site, resulted in two formations appearing directly in the chosen area, shrouded in mist - nothing was detected. The circle-making force is, as yet, elusive when it comes to being recorded in the act.

What Makes The Crop Circles And Why?

There are many different theories as to what might be behind these mysterious shapes in the crop fields, all with some apparent merit. The most popular theory amongst researchers is that they are created by some form of intelligence, either extra-terrestrial or from another dimension, and that they are the first steps in a communication process, using building blocks of symbolism which either make up some kind of language or connect with our subconscious minds in ways which we don't yet understand. (To begin with, some believed the marks were where flying saucers might have landed in the crop.) Others, notably Doug Ruby in his book *The Gift*, published in the US, have suggested that some of the shapes may be the blueprints for beneficial clean energy fields and propulsion devices to aid Mankind's development.

The crop circles seem to be attracted to particular areas, usually places where ancient sacred sites proliferate, such as stone circles and burial mounds. Those who practice the old art of 'dowsing' (where energies and objects can be detected with the aid of rods or pendulums) believe that the crop circles are very strong in 'earth energies', invisible lines of force which cover the planet, as are the ancient sites, and that they are attracted to form where these lines of energy meet, although this does not exclude the idea of intelligent manipulation being involved. Whatever creates the circles may well utilise this energy for its own purposes. England certainly seems to be the hub of crop circle activity and may be the 'energy centre' of the globe. The strength of earth energies apparently vary across the world and may be connected to the ability of local geological stratas to carry piezoelectric fields. Aquiferous rock, like chalk, which retains water, is particularly good for this and researcher Brian Grist has proposed in the journal *The Cerealogist* that this may explain why certain regions of England have more crop formations than others, as strips of aquiferous material notably run across some of the major circle-areas, including the prominent sites of Sussex (the maps in this book show clearly how many of the events seem to hug the line of the chalk South Downs). Individual formations are often found very close to underground water sources.

Others believe that the circles are created by the consciousness of the planet itself, Mother Earth, in conjunction with Nature Spirits and similar entities from the 'Devic' realms, as a form of warning that our abuse of the planet is about to result in catastrophe. The mystical and religious see the circles in a similarly apocalyptic vein, as part of the 'signs and wonders' which signpost the end of an era in human history.

Another theory gaining momentum is that the human mind itself may play a part in the process that results in these formations, or maybe it is the whole process, our expanding consciousness somehow interacting with the Earth's growing energy fields to create complex patterns thrown up by our subconscious minds. Certainly, the phenomenon has consistently demonstrated a capacity for knowing what is being thought about it. Someone, for instance, will think of a certain shape and location one day, only to find that shape impressed into the relevant field the next. Or someone else will declare a limiting boundary on the crop formations such as "The crop circles never do this..." and the very next day the phenomenon will do it. Sometimes the circle-making force seems to co-operate with attempted interaction; at other times it seems to delight in deliberately frustrating expectations.

Others believe that the patterns are made by unusual weather conditions, an idea prevalent in the early days of the phenomenon. In the light of the spectacular designs seen since, few now hold to this, although some believe that the simple circles are evidence for meteorological phenomena and that the more complex patterns are the work of pranksters. Alternatively, perhaps simple circles occur as natural phenomena and something has learnt to manipulate this force to create elaborate patterns.

Certainly, the most popular theory in the minds of the public is that the crop formations are simply made as a joke by people out for a bit of a laugh. Despite the constant attempt to reiterate this perception in the media, this is a view which doesn't stand up to scrutiny in the light of the circles' continuing presence and the mounting evidence that what is happening is a truly unexplained phenomenon. Clearly, there are a certain amount of man-made formations but it is increasingly apparent that such activity is only a very small part of the picture. If all the crop formations were made by people, there would have to be a dedicated purpose to it far beyond a joke and the people who have come forward to claim the phenomenon for their own would certainly not be the real minds behind it.

There are, of course, any number of other theories, ranging from sunspot activity to rutting hedgehogs. Perhaps the final answer is a combination of all of them. Or maybe none of them. The one thing that can safely be said for sure, is that no-one really knows. Some may believe they have the answers, but until definitive evidence comes along one way or the other, the best approach is simply to keep an open mind. Whatever the final answer, the crop circles are simply HERE, are beautiful and should be enjoyed while we have them. Perhaps it is their very mystery that is the fascination.

A Brief History Of The Phenomenon

Crop circles are generally recognised as a modern phenomenon but ongoing archival research and anecdotal evidence is beginning to reveal their presence in earlier times than previously thought. Some researchers believe the crop circles came in prehistoric eras and maybe were the templates for the erection of stone circles in some areas, but this can never be more than conjecture. If we discard the famous woodcut of 1678 which appears to show the Devil cutting a circular area of corn in a field, which some believe proves the existence of the circles as far back as then, the earliest reliable reports appear to be from the beginning of this century from people who grew up on farms and remember either seeing crop formations themselves as children or retain memory of relatives' stories of mysterious shapes appearing on their land.

But the emergence of the circle phenomenon as we now know it apparently began in earnest in the 1970s, with what became known as 'UFO nests' in Australia, small and simple circular areas of swirled grass and undergrowth discovered in the outback. Soon after these events, simple circles began to appear in the crop fields of England, principally in the area of what has now become known as the 'Wessex Triangle', a region of prolific crop circle activity covering Wiltshire and Hampshire. They attracted little attention beyond a few columns of curiosity in local newspapers but gave rise to the idea that perhaps some kind of weather phenomena could be responsible.

As time went on, these single circles began to get bigger and started to appear in groups, with several often in one field, and their distribution throughout the country began to expand into other counties. Small groups of people started to take notice of the phenomenon with more interest, especially Dr Terence Meaden, Colin Andrews and Pat Delgado, who began to document the appearance of crop circles in their spare time, visiting and recording them. Meaden believed implicitly that the weather was behind the circles and formulated his 'plasma vortex' theory of an electrically charged spinning column of air. Andrews and Delgado were not so sure and felt that some kind of premeditated element was involved. Subsequent events were to vindicate this feeling.

From the apparently random scatterings of previous circles, formations began to appear in geometrically precise patterns: a large circle would have, say, two others aligned perfectly either side of it, or three circles would appear grouped together in a triangular configuration. Most impressively, one of the first being at Alfriston in East Sussex, 'quintuplets' were discovered - a central circle surrounded by four smaller ones, equally placed liked dots on a dice. It was rapidly becoming clear that something far more complex and challenging than simple weather phenomena was at work, although proponents of the vortex theory continued to fine-tune their ideas to account for this new development of structured designs. By the mid 1980's, the crop circles were growing evermore numerous and their configurations more adventurous. When rings started appearing around circles, even double rings in some cases, and the complexity of the way the crop itself was laid down continued to surprise, there was no longer any doubt in the minds of many that something very special was happening in the fields of England.

With the publication of Andrews and Delgado's *Circular Evidence* in 1989 and its arrival on the best-sellers lists, the phenomenon exploded into the public eye and the media was suddenly full of speculation into what might be behind these huge and beautiful circles which appeared so mysteriously. By now, momentum had gained behind the idea that some kind of intelligence, probably extra-terrestrial, might be responsible for the circles, especially given the large numbers of lights in the sky being seen in connection with many formations. Strange sightings, sounds, and unusual effects were regularly being reported. Others, however, were becoming more sceptical.

When a circle appeared at Winterbourne Stoke, Wiltshire, in 1989, split into four quadrants of wheat flowed in different directions, the game was seemingly up for the weather-theorists. But it was 1990 which dealt the final blow, with the discovery of 'pictograms' - circles and rings linked by rectangular pathways in strange symbolic designs. From this point on, any shape could be expected to appear and invariably did - triangles, semi-circles, claw and key-type shapes, all in evermore imaginative combinations and ambitious sizes. Crop circles were now part of popular mythology and the huge formation which appeared at Alton Barnes in Wiltshire in the summer of 1990 hit the headlines in nearly every national newspaper, even prompting the rock group *Led Zeppelin* to adopt it for one of their album sleeves.

A number of people believe some in the higher echelons of authority were worried by the furore surrounding the circle phenomenon and the potential fear which could arise from such an uncontrollable mystery. They hold that this is one of the reasons why the idea that the crop circles might be nothing more than an elaborate human prank began to take on a higher profile from hereon. Some believe there was a concerted and co-ordinated effort from somewhere to publicly humiliate circle researchers and debunk the phenomenon. If true, the first evidence for this may have been the sabotaging of Colin Andrews' 'Operation Blackbird', which attempted to film a crop circle appearing with high-tech equipment and military assistance. Strange lights were observed by their cameras one night and a crop formation was found in the vicinity the next morning. This was given huge television coverage - only for the event to be revealed as a hoax later that day, with a mystic board game and a crucifix left in the centre of the formation to leave no room for doubt that people had been there. Somebody, somewhere, had, it seemed, carefully manipulated events to give a very public display that maybe all the crop formations were nothing more than the work of humans. Although damage was done, the public still wanted to believe the circles had a 'genuine' force behind them - it was not until a year later that another similar debunking exercise would be attempted, this time with more success.

In 1991 the phenomenon was even more astonishing, with the ever-growing numbers and complexity of formations, which were by now appearing in countries all over the world; America, Canada, Mexico, Brazil, Germany, Romania, Hungary, Switzerland, Belgium, Japan, to name but a few. The heart of the activity remained in England though, and two events in particular, a vast triangular design at Barbury Castle in Wiltshire and a 'Mandelbrot Set' at Ickleton in Cambridgeshire, shocked both the media and researchers with their breathtaking size, beauty and accuracy. The Mandelbrot design marked a significant step forward in being the first truly recognisable symbol to have appeared. A Mandelbrot Set, named after its discoverer Benoit Mandelbrot, is a shape which arises on computer screens when using specific type of 'fractal' equations, generated from reiterative mathematical sequences involving complex numbers. Many had remarked on the significant resemblance of certain formations to various symbols from cultures around the world before, but there was no doubt that the Mandelbrot was exactly what it appeared to be.

After such a summer of incredible circle activity, the phenomenon seemed immune to any scepticism that could destroy its reputation as something genuinely unexplained, however, at the end of the 1991 season, *Today* newspaper (now defunct) published a story that was to create lasting damage to the credibility of crop circles in the public eye. Two retired gentlemen from the Southampton area, Doug Bower and Dave Chorley, suddenly announced to the world that they had been responsible for making all the crop circles with nothing more sophisticated than a plank of wood on rope. They were reportedly tired of seeing "their" work being used to further the careers of so-called circle scientists, or 'cerealogists' as they by now called themselves, and were telling all to break the prank to the world at last. The media lapped it up; a good silly-season story with two loveable British eccentrics making fools of highbrow minds waxing lyrical over the huge significance of the crop circles. Everyone could relax - there were no strange forces at work in the fields after all, no potential threat or messages from superior intelligences, nothing that anyone had to concern themselves with anymore; just two old-age pensioners from Hampshire having a lark. A lark which, as several unconvinced researchers pointed out, must have been going on for a decade and a half - not to mention a century; quite a long time to keep a simple prank going.

It soon became apparent to anyone with detailed knowledge about the crop circle phenomenon and its history, that Doug and Dave's story didn't make sense. Not only were there gaping inconsistencies in their testimony, which changed to accommodate every challenge made to them, it was also clear that these two 'pranksters' simply didn't have the skill or draughtsman-like qualities that would have been needed to create the vast and intricately complex formations to which they were laying claim. A simple look at the vast amount which had appeared and the widespread geographic distribution of the circles revealed the impossibility of their story. Later experiments with man-made circles (a competition was held in 1992) showed that even small crop patterns took several hours to create in favourable daylight conditions. With many large formations often appearing on the same night over a wide area, how could Doug and Dave have worked so fast and so accurately? How were the growing numbers of overseas formations to be accounted for? How could their claims explain the many sightings of strange lights and other paranormal phenomena which had been experienced in connection with the circles? How had they achieved seemingly impossible effects in the crop itself?

As many questions began to arise, it was clear that Doug and Dave were not all they seemed. Almost no evidence had been produced to back up their claims. The demonstration formations they created for the media cameras were extremely messy and bore little relation to what experienced researchers were used to seeing. Most of these researchers realised very quickly that the public were being hoodwinked, but the damage had already been done. To this day, many believe that Doug and Dave were simply the tip of a concerted effort by higher authorities to deflate interest in the phenomenon, the culmination of a debunking campaign started at Operation Blackbird the year before. Whatever the case, the effect of this story coming forward was the same; most people were now quite happy to accept the crop circles as a joke and nothing more. As time went by, Doug and Dave admitted that they hadn't made all the circles but claimed that the remaining formations were made by other hoaxers imitating their handiwork!

With the two principle circle-makers apparently "retired", cerealogists were encouraged, but hardly surprised, to see the crop patterns back for 1992, with all the same effects and qualities witnessed in previous years, even if the designs were perhaps a little more subdued than they had been. Those who believed the formations had a link with human consciousness noted that as the circles always seemed to respond to expectations of them, perhaps, in the light of the much scaled-down interest as a result of Doug and Dave, the phenomenon was simply responding in kind. One good effect the lessened public interest resulted in was that genuine researchers found their work less interrupted by sensation-seeking sightseers. Everyone out documenting the phenomenon was there because they really believed they were still dealing with something special. New sceptics and supposed circle hoaxers crawled out of the woodwork in an attempt to cash in on the Doug and Dave bonanza with as little evidence or credentials as their predecessors. An entire sub-culture sprang up in the Wessex Triangle, particularly at Alton Barnes in Wiltshire, of enthusiasts and debunkers, each trying to catch the other out. Thus the term 'croppie' was born to replace the rather formal 'cerealogist' which became reserved for the more serious-minded circle-scholar. By now it was clear that the crop circles - and the aura of interest and enthusiasm surrounding them, if a little more select than before - were not going to go away.

1993 began to see the crop circles creep back into the public awareness with the realisation that strange things were still happening in the fields. The formations themselves began to get bolder again in design and numbers, culminating in the last of the season at Bythorn in Cambridgeshire. This formation resembled a beautiful flower or mandala, with ten petals surrounding rings and a pentacle, and marked a shift in the style of designs which pointed the way for things to come. What was unusual about the pattern was that much of its design was made up from crop still standing on a bed of flattened plants, a reversal of the usual pattern etched inwards into the field. This new style would become almost commonplace in the next two years.

The expectations raised by the Bythorn mandala were not disappointed in 1994, which turned out to be probably the best year for the phenomenon yet witnessed, despite the media's insistence that no crop circles were appearing anymore! Wiltshire in particular simply exploded with designs of staggering complexity and imaginative flair. By now, everyone agreed that whatever the source behind the crop circles, whether a superior intelligence, natural force or people, they were sheer works of

The vastness of some formations is not always appreciated from a distance. Inside, the sense of scale can be breathtaking, as demonstrated at this formation at Upper Beeding in 1995 (95/12). Photo: Andy Thomas.

genius and an artform of the highest level. Of the many different shapes being found, the most impressive were the 'galaxies', spiral-armed flattened circles with standing clumps which seemed to represent stars and planets, the 'scorpions' or 'thought bubbles', long formations made up of many circles diminishing in size like tails, and the increasingly ambitious crescent moon designs which had first began to appear in 1992. Even long-term sceptics were forced to admit that these formations were difficult to explain in terms of people perpetrating a practical joke and supposed self-confessed 'hoaxers' began to talk in terms of simply adding to an existing phenomenon instead of being the phenomenon.

The following year was a very hot and dry summer and consequently the harvest was brought in very early, which perhaps explains why there were fewer English events in 1995, although by now crop formations were appearing in huge numbers around the world. The ones which did appear in England were no less impressive than their ancestors though and the recurring theme for the year seemed to be 'asteroids' - rings made up from many different-sized small circles, usually surrounding designs of orbiting planets. The circle - the very shape which had started the phenomenon off in the first place - seemed to reassert itself as the predominant element of the crop formations, after some of the bizarre variations which had been seen in 1994. After the hugely prolific appearances in Wiltshire the year before, there was a curious shift of location for the majority of formations which appeared. For the first time since it all began, Wiltshire was virtually ignored by the circle-making force, and other counties which had previously been privileged to have at least a few visits from the phenomenon were mysteriously missed altogether - except Sussex, which had another bumper year, making Sussex the second most circle-visited county after Hampshire, which was given the majority of the year's spectacular designs.

Sussex has always done well in terms of numbers of crop circles, and has been host to some of the more interesting formations and events, which it is this book's purpose to document. With this resume of the overall saga of the crop circles in our minds, the following chapters slot into place the important part Sussex has played in the development of this most amazing phenomenon.

THE EARLY YEARS

Ref: 43/01
Location: Tangmere, West Sussex
Map Ref: 910 060
Date: Summer 1943

Ref: 84/02
Location: Wick Street, East Sussex
Map Ref: 543 084
Date: Summer 1984

Ref: E70/01
Location: Patcham, East Sussex
Map Ref: 307 096
Date: Early 1970's

Ref: 85/01
Location: Findon, West Sussex
Map Ref: 102 087
Date: Summer 1985

Ref: M80/01
Location: Falmer, East Sussex
Map Ref: 362 072
Date: Mid-1980's

Ref: 74/01
Location: Falmer, East Sussex
Map Ref: 362 072
Date: Summer 1974

Ref: 86/01
Location: Alfriston, East Sussex
Map Ref: 495 027
Date: 10/7/86

Ref: 89/01
Location: Lewes, East Sussex
Map Ref: 392 096
Date: Summer 1989

Ref: 84/01
Location: Alfriston, East Sussex
Map Ref: 512 015
Date: 27/7/84

Ref: 89/02
Location: Bishopstone, East Sussex
Map Ref: 475 015
Date: Summer 1989

THE EARLY YEARS

From two possible crop formations in the Second World War to the summer of 1989, Sussex was quietly active with the phenomenon long before any public attention was raised towards the circles...

1943: The Earliest Sussex Formations..?

In the summer of 1995, the Dorset-based crop circle researcher David Kingston stepped down from the stage after giving a presentation to an audience hungry for circle-information at Bognor Regis, and was instantly swamped by people wanting to talk. Among this crowd was a solitary figure bearing an envelope, who, in the few minutes he was able to have David's attention, opened it and divulged its astonishing contents. From the envelope he produced several old black and white photographs, allegedly taken from the air above the RAF base at Tangmere, near Chichester, in the late summer of 1943. Tangmere was an important airbase during the Second World War, and many aerial shots of the surrounding landscape were taken. The photographs purported to be from these records.

In the pictures, two perfect circles (43/01) could be very clearly seen lying in a field of crop very close to RAF Tangmere, each about 20' to 30' across. There were none of the tractor 'tramline' markings we have come to expect crossing the fields and no visible trails through the crop where anyone had entered the field to investigate. The photographs certainly seemed authentic, taken in an old square-shaped format used in those days.

Unfortunately, in the melee of people trying to talk to David Kingston, the gentleman with these photographs slipped away without leaving any contact address. He has not been heard from since. In an effort to track down copies of these pictures, David contacted the Air Ministry Museum who hold all such records of photographs taken during the war, but they advised him that they did not hold copies. Unless the photos showed anything of 'official interest', they would not have been kept but instead given away or destroyed.

If genuine, these pictures are the earliest photographic references of the crop circle phenomenon ever recorded anywhere. There are a growing number of accounts of crop formations from the earlier part of the 20th century, although study of archive aerial photographs has, as yet, yielded no evidence - until now. Many believe the circles have been with us for far longer than we have so far been aware. It would seem that Sussex was one of the first areas to become active with the appearance of these mysterious shapes in the fields - although another three decades were to pass before anyone began to take notice. Little is known of many of the formations which appeared in the early years of the phenomenon in Sussex, but research and anecdotal evidence has enabled the following information to be documented...

The 1970's

Thirty years after the Tangmere events, the first two formations to be noted in the memory of observers were to occur in the first half of the 1970's.

While investigating a formation which appeared at Patcham, near Brighton, in 1991, the farmer remarked to researcher Barry Reynolds that he remembered a single circle appearing on his land back in the "early 1970's" (E70/01). It was apparently well-formed and very flat to the ground, and was found in the fields at the back of Patcham which head out north towards the beauty spot of Ditchling Beacon. This location puts it very close to where Sussex was to have its first oilseed rape formation in the summer of 1994.

Not very far from Patcham, two brothers, Bob and Peter Powell from Lewes, remember seeing a single circle in 1974, while riding in their parents' car, from the road going out to Woodingdean from Falmer, in the fields looking west towards Lewes (74/01).

The Famous Quintuplet Of '84

One of the most famous crop circles in Sussex has become the formation which appeared ten years after the Woodingdean sighting, in an area which would become a cherished site for the circle-making forces - the picturesque village of Alfriston, a few miles north of Seaford. The fame of the pattern (84/01) which appeared in wheat on the 27th July 1984 was due both to its complex configuration (for the time) and to the status of a gentleman who was to photograph it - the Labour MP Denis Healey, now Lord Healey of Riddlesden.

Up until now, most of the few crop formations appearing around the country were simple circles, with occasional pairs or groups being found. But the event at Alfriston was one of the most advanced kind - a central circle orbited by four smaller ones spaced at regular intervals - a quintuplet. This was one of the first of its type to be discovered,

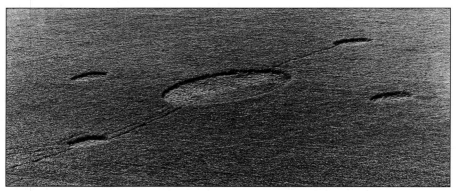

The Quintuplet at Alfriston, 1984 (84/01), one of the most advanced designs of its time. The unsightly pathways were probably made by visitors – reportedly, the circles were not originally joined.
Photo: John Holloway.

preceded only by two rare quintuplets in Hampshire in 1983 and 1978. The Alfriston area had long been associated with sightings of unusual lights in the sky and even the Police reported seeing glowing objects in the sky at nearby Hindover in the later part of the 1980's. The farmer who owned the field was reportedly a little scared at the implications of the shape which had flattened his crop.

It was about this time that crop circles were beginning to attract some minor attention from the media and the Alfriston formation was the first Sussex event to appear in the local press, most prominently in the *Sussex Express*, which was to sporadically report on circles in East Sussex thereafter.

The quintuplet formation had the good fortune (if indeed it was coincidence) to appear in fields very close to the home of Denis Healey, a prominent politician and a respected amateur photographer. Knowing little as to the origins of the strange design which stared up from the fields towards his house, Denis nevertheless realised that here was something worth recording for posterity and photographed it. A few weeks later, his pictures somehow came to the attention of the national tabloid press and suddenly the news of the formation, given credence by its connection to a celebrity, was splashed across a page of the *Daily Mail* newspaper. This turned out to be an important development in the dawning awareness of the public to the circles phenomenon, being one of the first occasions where crop circles were prominently displayed and questions were asked as to their origins.

In the same year, 1984, not very far from Alfriston, a very small single circle appeared in uncultivated long grass at Wick Street, near Arlington (84/02). Very close to the northerly part of the Cuckmere river, which runs very thin here, a 7' circle, spiralled clockwise, appeared on the edge of a field near the riverbank. The respected dowser and circle researcher David Tilt, who was alerted to the formation's appearance after dowsing the Alfriston quintuplet, believes this location, together with several others in the general area (especially the ancient mound near Berwick church), used to be the site of an old henge erected in Neolithic times.

The Rest Of The 80's

Another early and excellent example of a quintuplet set appeared the year after its Sussex predecessor, in 1985, at Findon, near Worthing (85/01). Clouds of 'steam' were seen rising from the field the morning of its discovery. This formation managed to attract the attention of the *Worthing Gazette* newspaper, making its name on the front cover with an accompanying photograph and was eventually reported in the *Daily Express*.

The circle phenomenon then returned to Alfriston once again, albeit with less publicity, on the 10th July 1986 (86/01), very close to the location of the quintuplet two years previously. This time, two circles, one 30' and the other 15', appeared together in one field in young green crop which recovered very quickly. When crop is still strong and unripe, it will often quickly stand up again after having been flattened, which is why formations which arrive earlier in the summer often appear rougher than those later in the season.

The only other event known about during this mid-80's period is word of one which appeared at Falmer, near Brighton, year and configuration unknown (M80/01). A farmer in the area, on learning of a neighbouring farm's formation which appeared there in 1990, remarked that he had something similar on his land about five years earlier. Sometimes, such vague memories are all that remain to be recorded for posterity!

Often, earlier formations are learnt of through people's comments in relation to contemporary ones. This is how it is known, for instance, that one was found in 1989 at Houndean Bottom in Lewes, the County Town of East Sussex (89/01). Tom Fenn, who discovered the Lewes pictogram of 1990, is quoted in the *Sussex Express* from that year as saying "My brother stumbled on one at the same place last year"... James Fenn and his wife were walking along the footpath across the top of the field and spotted a single circle in the crop.

The last 80's formation known about to date, probably another single circle, appeared at Bishopstone, near Seaford, in the summer of 1989 (89/02), details again unknown. With the growing publicity given to the crop circle phenomenon at the end of the decade and the start of the next, especially with the arrival of the 'pictograms' in 1990, more people began to notice the bizarre and wonderful events going on around them and known details of crop formations became a little more comprehensive as these people started to actively seek out the crop circles...

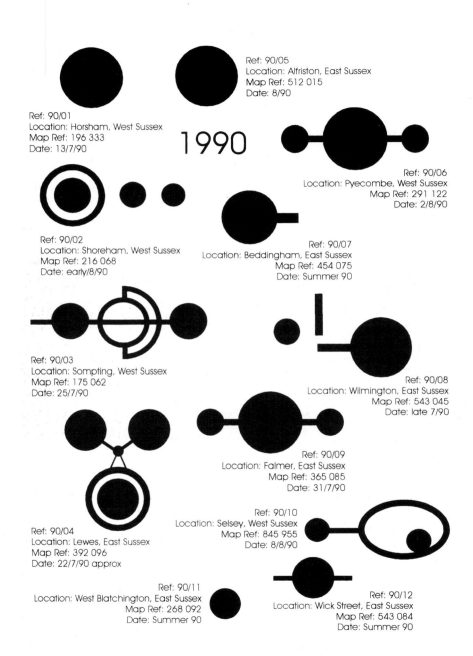

Ref: 90/01
Location: Horsham, West Sussex
Map Ref: 196 333
Date: 13/7/90

Ref: 90/05
Location: Alfriston, East Sussex
Map Ref: 512 015
Date: 8/90

1990

Ref: 90/06
Location: Pyecombe, West Sussex
Map Ref: 291 122
Date: 2/8/90

Ref: 90/02
Location: Shoreham, West Sussex
Map Ref: 216 068
Date: early/8/90

Ref: 90/07
Location: Beddingham, East Sussex
Map Ref: 454 075
Date: Summer 90

Ref: 90/03
Location: Sompting, West Sussex
Map Ref: 175 062
Date: 25/7/90

Ref: 90/08
Location: Wilmington, East Sussex
Map Ref: 543 045
Date: late 7/90

Ref: 90/09
Location: Falmer, East Sussex
Map Ref: 365 085
Date: 31/7/90

Ref: 90/04
Location: Lewes, East Sussex
Map Ref: 392 096
Date: 22/7/90 approx

Ref: 90/10
Location: Selsey, West Sussex
Map Ref: 845 955
Date: 8/8/90

Ref: 90/11
Location: West Blatchington, East Sussex
Map Ref: 268 092
Date: Summer 90

Ref: 90/12
Location: Wick Street, East Sussex
Map Ref: 543 084
Date: Summer 90

1990

As the crop circle phenomenon exploded in numbers and in the amount of publicity received around the country, so too did the Sussex formations, which multiplied and grew bolder in their design.

A Quiet Beginning

The first formation to be recorded in 1990 gave little indication of the extraordinary season it was beginning. As Wiltshire began having some of the most incredible designs ever seen, the phenomenon taking a quantum leap with the development of the pictogram configurations, Sussex started quietly with a single 60' circle in wheat (90/01) just above Horsham, on the by-pass which goes through Warnham to Crawley, from which direction it could be seen clearly from the road. It appeared on the 13th July and was rather more oval than circular.

The first circle of the year as seen from the Horsham by-pass (90/01). Photo: Martin Noakes.

The First Sussex Pictograms

On 25th July, Sussex was treated to its first pictogram, very reminiscent of the designs Wiltshire had been seeing, at Sompting, north of Worthing. Few realised at the time that this formation (90/03) was opening up the first chapter of a saga which would continue in this area for years to come. Instead of just the combination of simple circles which had been seen in Sussex fields so far, here was a formation constructed of many shapes: two circles, linked with a long rectangular pathway around which ran a ring between the two circles, which in turn had a semi-circular ring around it, forming a kind of arch. All parts were flowed anticlockwise.

The formation, in wheat, was very well laid with extremely clean-cut edges and appeared only 100' or so from the back of a row of houses which edged the field. Neighbours heard and saw nothing the night it appeared. The overall length was about 160'. The dowser David Russell found very strong earth energy imprints in this formation - which remain in the ground to this day despite the formation being long-since vanished. Dowsers believe the whole area of fields behind Sompting is alive with this energy, which the many patterns which were to appear here in subsequent years were to feed on in ways that became clearer as time went on.

At around the same date, another elaborate formation appeared at Houndean Bottom, on the eastern outskirts of Lewes (90/04), again in wheat. It appeared on exactly the same spot as the circle the year before, in the large sloping field which overlooks the roundabout filtering traffic into Lewes from the A27, but was on the brow of the field and was not visible from the road. Consisting of a ringed circle, this was topped with two small circles of about 20' connected by a V shape of pathways to an even smaller circle. Two pathways linking these to the main ringed circle appeared later although these might have been tracks where people walked. The crop was laid clockwise.

The formation was spotted from an aeroplane by Tom Fenn, a local amateur photographer, whose picture was to appear as the front cover story of the *Sussex Express*. Tom, together with five friends - one of whom was the drummer of the famous rock band AC/DC - later went into the formation one night and, on a inspiration, decided to have each person stand at points around its perimeter. As they began to walk together slowly, some of them simultaneously experienced a jolt of energy, like electricity, go up the back of their legs. David Tilt believes it was those who had been standing on the north-south points from the small circle at the centre who experienced the shock as they felt the flow of strong earth energies go through them.

David Tilt himself spent a lot of time dowsing the Lewes pictogram and found the atmosphere in there very oppressive. It was the most potent circle he remembers ever working on. A strange sulphur-like smell seemed to be present inside and David felt drained of energy and experienced headaches for three days. While David worked inside the circle, a curious event occurred: A Landrover entered the field at the bottom and drove straight across the crop! It pulled up inside the formation and two "important looking people" got out. Looking very serious and without saying a word to David they glanced around the circles, got back into the car, and drove back across the crop, never to be seen again.

By this time, several researchers had noted the many examples of crop patterns which were appearing very close to the location of ancient sacred sites, which may be due to the very strong earth energies present at these places, energies which inspired ancient man to mark these places with monuments or settlements. The first prominent example of this in Sussex was the formation which appeared a few fields north of the famous and ancient 'Long Man' chalk carving which gazes out across the village of Wilmington. This beautiful area has long been associated with mystical events and strange goings-on and the configuration in barley which appeared there (90/08) in late July was no exception to this pattern.

Its shape was certainly weird, a disjointed collection of a single circle, a thin rectangle and a large circle with a rectangular pathway emanating from it, all at odd angles to each other and unconnected. The farmer delayed harvesting the field to allow a few researchers in to view the formation. The lay of the crop was rough, although barley often doesn't lay as flat as other crops when pushed down and generally gives a messier appearance. The circular parts flowed anticlockwise. The patterns, not far from Wilmington Priory, appeared to be on the crossing point of two earth energy lines, marked exactly by the central rectangle, according to David Tilt.

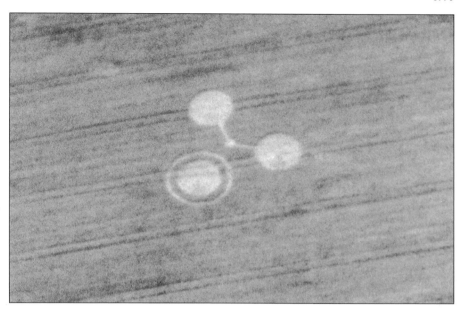

The Lewes pictogram (90/04) at Houndean Bottom. Photo: Tom Fenn.

A visitor examines the Lewes pictogram (90/04). The downs in the background are Kingston Ridge from where an eye-witness sighting of a circle being formed would be made in 1991. Photo: Tom Fenn.

One of these same energy lines led directly to another formation of 1990 which formed in July, a tiny circle back at Wick Street (90/12), which had seen a circle in 1984 on exactly the same spot. This time, the formation was a clockwise circle of 10' in wheat, rough and indistinct, with the vague hint of two rectangular pathways emanating from each side.

Some reports speak of another formation appearing back at the old haunt of Alfriston in 1990 (90/05), but confusion reigns as to whether this apparent single circle really did exist. The Brighton-based newspaper the *Evening Argus*, which occasionally reported some of the Sussex events, printed a brief article on crop circles on 8th August and referred to a circle at Alfriston. However, the accompanying photograph actually showed a picture of an unknown formation which the newspaper had already printed in 1989! It is possible that this report has become confused with accounts of the Wick Street 1990 circle.

Advent Of The Triplets

The first in a series of identical pictograms which would appear over the next two years arrived in wheat at Falmer on July 31st, directly below the sliproad which approaches

A combine harvester prepares to eat the triplet formation at Falmer (90/09), as seen from the sliproad to the University of Brighton buildings. Photo: Veronica Lenihan.

the University of Brighton buildings (90/09). Discovered by the farmers on their return from holiday, the formation was a chain of three circles in a row linked with thin pathways, the central circle larger than the outer ones. The circles measured 12', 24' and 6'. The crop had been laid down very neatly. David Tilt recalls that, like the Lewes pictogram, there was a curious "smell you could taste" that was only noticeable within the formation.

The next in the triplet series was discovered on 2nd August at Pyecombe (90/06), just above the A23 service station and was virtually indistinguishable in design from the Falmer pictogram. Aligned exactly east/west, it could be seen clearly from the road. All three circles, 14', 39' and 12', were laid anticlockwise and the total length of the formation was 91'.

This was the first Sussex formation to come to the attention of Barry Reynolds who

The triplet at Pyecombe (90/06). The A23 lies at the foot of the field. Photo: Sussex Express

was to be instrumental in the setting up of the Centre for Crop Circle Studies Sussex branch a year later. Returning from a pilgrimage to Wiltshire to experience the huge Alton Barnes pictogram which had been splashed across the national press, Barry was alerted to this local event while at work by a telephone call from his wife Linda. So excited was he by this news that he left his office on the spot to head out for the

Circles and rings at Mill Hill, Shoreham (90/02). A nearby resident charged people for a similar view from their garden! Photo: David Russell.

formation, which was the first he surveyed. The *Sussex Express* accidentally reported it as being at Ditchling.

A triplet of a different kind appeared at Mill Hill, Shoreham, in the first week of August (90/02). In a field directly north of the A27, not far from the huge Adur flyover junction, a large ringed circle was found, accompanied by two smaller circles in a row. Somebody in a house over the other side of the A27 must have had a good view of the formation from their garden - there are reports that in one of the nearby houses someone was charging people money to use their back garden as a viewing area! Little did anyone realise that this field would be visited twice more in subsequent years by the circle-making force. Perhaps the attraction to this field has a connection with the site of an old Bronze Age settlement which lies nearby.

Southerly Circles

The pictogram which appeared at Selsey on 8th August (90/10) holds the honour of being the most geographically southern formation to be found in Sussex yet (followed closely by the Birling Gap ovals discovered in 1994). Selsey sits on a little spur sticking out into the waters of the English Channel. The event itself was unknowingly hidden away in the catalogues of researcher Colin Andrews' database until a German croppie, Wolfgang Schindler, alerted CCCS Sussex to it in 1993. Aerial shots revealed the pictogram to be an interesting shape, a distinct oval ring with a small circle 'resting' on the inside like an eye, with a pathway from the ring leading to another small circle, however, its construction appeared very rough.

Stragglers...

Two more formations are known to have appeared in 1990, the year which had seen a most incredible leap forward for the phenomenon in Sussex. There is mention in the book *Circles From The Sky*, edited by Terence Meaden, of a "single spurred circle" near Beddingham, between Lewes and Newhaven (90/07). One must assume from this description some kind of single circle with an emanating short rectangular pathway.

When investigating the formation at West Blatchington in 1992, CCCS Sussex learnt from the farmer of a 12' single circle which appeared near the golf club which operates there (90/11), although there is a possibility this may have occurred in 1989.

1990 had been astonishing... 1991 was to be even more so, the designs taking on a more regulated form, and would see interest growing in the crop circle phenomenon from yet more individuals in Sussex who were beginning to study these strange but compelling shapes which were flowering everywhere without explanation.

David Tilt dowses the Wilmington formation of 1990 (90/08) as the field is harvested around him, with the Long Man hill figure in the distance. Photo: Sussex Express.

Inside the Falmer triplet (90/09). Photo: Veronica Lenihan

1991

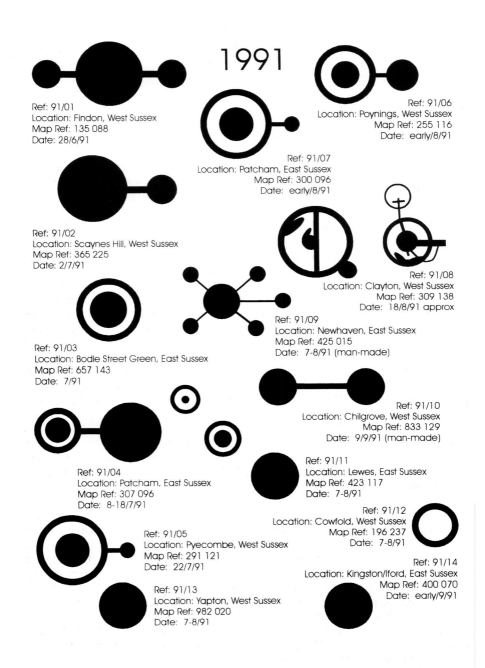

Ref: 91/01
Location: Findon, West Sussex
Map Ref: 135 088
Date: 28/6/91

Ref: 91/02
Location: Scaynes Hill, West Sussex
Map Ref: 365 225
Date: 2/7/91

Ref: 91/03
Location: Bodle Street Green, East Sussex
Map Ref: 657 143
Date: 7/91

Ref: 91/04
Location: Patcham, East Sussex
Map Ref: 307 096
Date: 8-18/7/91

Ref: 91/05
Location: Pyecombe, West Sussex
Map Ref: 291 121
Date: 22/7/91

Ref: 91/06
Location: Poynings, West Sussex
Map Ref: 255 116
Date: early/8/91

Ref: 91/07
Location: Patcham, East Sussex
Map Ref: 300 096
Date: early/8/91

Ref: 91/08
Location: Clayton, West Sussex
Map Ref: 309 138
Date: 18/8/91 approx

Ref: 91/09
Location: Newhaven, East Sussex
Map Ref: 425 015
Date: 7-8/91 (man-made)

Ref: 91/10
Location: Chilgrove, West Sussex
Map Ref: 833 129
Date: 9/9/91 (man-made)

Ref: 91/11
Location: Lewes, East Sussex
Map Ref: 423 117
Date: 7-8/91

Ref: 91/12
Location: Cowfold, West Sussex
Map Ref: 196 237
Date: 7-8/91

Ref: 91/13
Location: Yapton, West Sussex
Map Ref: 982 020
Date: 7-8/91

Ref: 91/14
Location: Kingston/Iford, East Sussex
Map Ref: 400 070
Date: early/9/91

1991

The 'Sussex Dumbbell' makes its appearance, an eye-witness watches a circle form before his eyes, and Doug and Dave cross the border for the cameras…

The Triplet Returns

Back at Findon, which had played host to one of the early quintuplets in 1985, the familiar triplet design of three linked circles in a row opened the 1991 season on 28th June (91/01). Found in barley, each circle measured approximately 30' and flowed anticlockwise. The overall length of the formation was 110'. To anyone's knowledge, this was the earliest a formation had been discovered in Sussex at this time. This date was to be continually pushed back each successive year onwards, until in 1995 one was to appear in the second week of May.

Dawning Of The Sussex Dumbbell

On 2nd July at Scaynes Hill, near Haywards Heath, a crop design appeared which was to haunt the fields of Sussex again and again in 1991. Whereas the formations elsewhere in the country were growing evermore ambitious and diverse, the local pictograms took on more of a uniformity with the arrival of what were to become known as the 'Sussex dumbbells'; variations on the theme of a large circle, sometimes ringed, with a short straight path leading to a smaller circle. This shape had been seen in other parts of the country, but not as prolifically as in Sussex this season. This first example at Scaynes Hill (91/02) was not ringed and appeared in wheat, the main circle being 55' and the small 30'. The overall length was 95'.

The next example of this design (91/04) was found together with two other formations - ringed circles - in the same field, at Patcham, near Brighton, site of one of the early 1970's circles. The field was visited by the circle-making force on four separate nights over a period of ten days between the 8th and 18th July, resulting in an impressive spectacle of three formations scattered across a single meadow of golden barley. This was the most adventurous behaviour the crop circles had yet exhibited in Sussex. The main circle of the dumbbell - this time with the small circle ringed - was 54' and had a 15' pathway leading to the small 15' ringed circle. The two isolated ringed circles were never surveyed.

The field was directly next to where the new stretch of the A27 Brighton by-pass was being excavated, at this point still a chalk strip. Just over the brow of the hill to the west were the road builders' huts and caravans. There were reports that some of the workmen heard strange noises and witnessed small glowing lights in the sky above the field on the nights the three formations gradually appeared. The A27 and the siting of crop circles in alignment with it was to take on a greater significance the following year and prompt speculation as to the implications.

The following three events would be the dumbbell shapes alone, but with the main circles ringed. The first of these, but of a more squat design than the first Patcham one, appeared at Pyecombe in the same field as its predecessor the year before (91/05). Discovered in wheat on 22nd July, the outer ring of the main circle was 75' and the little circle was 14', total length 112'. All the swirls flowed anticlockwise.

On 17th July, Barry Reynolds, who was by now, as were a number of others this year,

The Pyecombe dumbbell with the chalk strip of the new A23 carriageway in construction below it. New road developments seem to attract the circle phenomenon in Sussex. Photo: Barry Reynolds.

A good example of the 'Sussex dumbbell' at Poynings (91/06). Visitors have again defaced the field by not walking up the tractor tramlines.
Photo: Andy Thomas.

actively scouring the fields for formations, made a curious and uncanny prediction with regard to this. A Venture Scout leader, Barry was driving a minibus of Venture Scouts down the A23, and, on the spur of the moment as they passed the site of the Pyecombe formation of the previous year, he announced that another would appear in a certain place in the same field within seven to ten days. Amazingly, only five days later, one of the girls who had been on the bus spotted the new dumbbell shape when driving past the same spot. It was in exactly the area of the field where Barry had indicated a formation would appear! This story was typical of other such reports which were growing more numerous around the country, indicating that some kind of psychic interaction between humans and the crop circles appeared to be taking place.

After local press reports about the Pyecombe event, a motorist contacted the newspapers to say that he had witnessed people making the dumbbell. In fact, after dates and times were examined, it transpired that what he had seen was Barry Reynolds and his friends measuring and surveying it... Survey teams are often mistakenly taken for people making crop formations instead of measuring them.

One of the best examples of the Sussex dumbbell was discovered at Poynings (91/06), at the northern foot of the South Downs in early August. A very good view could be had from the path going west from the car park at the top of Devil's Dyke. The formation was very clear-cut but had a number of unusual and very thin pathways splaying out from the ringed circle, trickling off into the crop as if a "burst of energy", as David Russell described it, had splattered out from it. All parts of the formation flowed anticlockwise. Unfortunately its pristineness was soon worn down because of its high visibility and sightseers carved unsightly pathways across the field instead of using the tractor tramlines, a common problem when enthusiasm gets in the way of sense. By 1991, this increasing sort of behaviour (by people who probably hadn't sought permission to enter the field in the first place) was not exactly helping to endear farmers to the presence of crop formations.

The last of the dumbbell shapes for 1991 was again found at Patcham in wheat (91/07), this time in the field directly overlooking the A27 workmen's caravans and the new junction with the existing A23 from Brighton to London, opposite Sweet Hill. It appeared the same week as the Poynings event and was identical to the squat shape of the Pyecombe dumbbell. This time no reports were made of any unusual lights or sound.

Other Configurations

The Sussex dumbbell didn't make up all of the 1991 formations. Back in July, a 51' ringed circle in wheat (91/03) was discovered by a farmer at Bodle Street Green, near Herstmonceux, while he was harvesting a field. In a dramatic break with the growing tradition of circle-hatred from some farmers across the country, the farmer found himself unable to desecrate the beautiful shape he had found and cut around it instead. He then informed the local people from the village of his find and invited them into his field to look! Some of the reports indicate that a small 'grapeshot' circle was also found in the same field.

Around the 18th August, two far more elaborate but crudely made configurations were found at Clayton, at the foot of the downs where the twin windmills 'Jack and Jill' stand (91/08). One appeared to be a rough estimation of the now classic dumbbell shape but with a pathway emanating from the centre of the ringed circle to outside the oddly-proportioned ring. About 70' to the west was another strange ring with a line through its middle and various odd shapes around it. Perched on the outside of the ring was a single oval. Other crude markings were dotted around the field. The lay of the crop was also rough. All parts of the formations flowed clockwise except the small ring of the dumbbell, which was anticlockwise. Dowsing appeared to show them as being on an energy line coming directly from Clayton church. The farmer who owned the field later made reference to another formation on his land which was found in 1991 but nothing is known of its whereabouts or design.

The Circle Remains The Same

Despite the evolution of the designs over the last few seasons, one shape remained constant; the single circle. With all the elaborate pictograms and diversity, simple, and often small, circles continued to appear but in the light of the more interesting things going on they received far less publicity. By this time, those who believed that the crop formations were the result of rare weather vortices pointed to the consistent appearance of these circles as proof of the real phenomenon continuing whereas the complicated patterns were man-made in their opinion. The fact that the same effects in the way the crops were laid down were being discovered in both single circles and pictograms seemed to escape their attention.

At the end of July and the beginning of August, two of these single circles appeared, one near Malling Brooks at Lewes (91/11) and another at Yapton, near Arundel (91/13). Almost nothing is known of the Lewes formation, information about which came from a student who, by chance, attended the same college as a group who were involved in creating a rough hoax at Newhaven. Crop circles came up in conversation between students and a teacher at a Sussex-based college, in discussion as to whether or not the phenomenon could be attributable to human activity. The debate wound up with the teacher (somewhat irresponsibly) encouraging the students to go out and have a go at making a formation themselves! The results of their efforts appeared in the fields just outside the coastal town of Newhaven, a circle with five spidery arms ending in small splurgey circles (91/09). The students themselves were the first to admit that their

Circle at Yapton (91/13), as photographed from the cab of a combine harvester. Photo: Anon.

handiwork was not impressive... Their arguments came down much more in favour of a non-human cause behind the circles as a result!

The Yapton circle was discovered by the farmers while harvesting the field. Some formations aren't discovered until this point and it's quite likely that several are cut down each year without any knowledge of them reaching the outside world. On this occasion, the farmers were, like their counterpart at Bodle Street Green, sufficiently enthused to stop the combines and photograph the 30' circle. The lay of the crop was very even and smooth and the farmers, who grew most of their crops organically, were excited at the presence of the circle on their land.

One more single circle (91/14) appeared - literally - in 1991 in extraordinary circumstances, as we shall see. Other than this, the last of the small circular events to occur was at Cowfold, where a tiny single ring of 10' was discovered (91/12).

Doug And Dave's Day Out

At the very end of the season, on 9th September, when nearly every crop field around the country had been harvested, one was left standing at Chilgrove, near the border with Hampshire, deliberately, one assumes, so that the two 'naughty boys' Doug and Dave, who had just broken their we-made-all-the-circles story to the press, could show off their 'handiwork' to the cameras for the first time. Thus Sussex once again, if dubiously this time, played a major role in the history of the crop circles. The farmer was paid for the damage to the crop and damage was about the only description one could give to the appalling mess they created in front of television crews, which was a crude dumbbell shape with a long pathway between two similar size circles (91/10). The lay was so rough that anyone who knew the real excellence that was being found inside most of the crop designs appearing all over the country could immediately see that these two elderly men could not possibly have been responsible for what they claimed. By breaking their story so late in the year, Doug and Dave, or whatever agency was responsible for them, ensured that no other formations could appear that year for comparison. However, one or two fields did remain standing... In any case, the damage to the credibility of crop circles was done, for now at least, although few researchers in Sussex were to be put off.

An Eye-Witness Account

As if in response to the challenge laid down by the Doug and Dave gauntlet to the validity of the circles as a genuinely unexplained phenomenon, an event occurred in the same week, at the beginning of September, which was to balance the situation perfectly although knowledge of it was not to come to light until a few years later.

Many researchers had tried, in vain, to film or be witness to the creation of a crop formation appearing in front of their very eyes. Every attempt at achieving this had failed. However, a growing number of accounts from people who were not connected with researching the phenomenon showed that the creation of crop circles had been witnessed on occasion, most notably by Vivienne and Gary Tomlinson, a married couple from Surrey who claimed to have had one of two circles connected by a zig-zag path actually form around them in a matter of seconds. Perhaps the very intent to find a time and a place where a circle would form was enough to prevent it happening; the phenomenon remained elusive when it came to being caught in the act by those who wished it. It was surely no coincidence that the people who were witnessing the formation of crop circles were those who neither knew nor cared about the phenomenon.

Martin Sohn-Rethel was no exception to this, knowing little more about crop circles than what had appeared in the news. A college tutor, Martin and his family had recently moved down from Dorset to the village of Kingston, near Lewes, and were exploring the downs which overlook Kingston, Swanborough and Iford one sunny

Sunday afternoon when an extraordinary thing happened. Martin admits that his memory of events is now hazy, but one thing is certain - he watched a crop circle appear in a field.

The weather that day was very clear and warm when Martin, his wife, three children and another child (a friend) set out onto the downs in the early afternoon. As they walked along the paths which follow the line of the downs, they found themselves above the meadows between the hamlets of Swanborough and Iford. As Martin gazed inland across the fields, one of which, about 30 yards away, had not yet been harvested, a strange and very strong gust of wind began to blow. Where they stood, the air was still. He watched, more with detached interest than amazement, as this 'wind' appeared to cross into the field of standing crop.

Suddenly, in no more than "five to ten seconds", about 20 yards in from the northern edge of the field, a perfect circle simply appeared in the crop as Martin watched, as if a vortex of air had spun the stems down. There were no unusual lights or sounds, just the apparent movement of air. Only Martin was watching the field when the circle formed. Instead of the incredulous reaction many might have had to this event, his initial thoughts were about how angry the farmer would be on finding his field damaged! Martin estimates the circle must have been about 40', but can't recall the type of crop in the field.

After the circle had appeared, the odd localised wind which had apparently created it moved up the field and towards the Sohn-Rethel family where they were buffeted by it. Dust and stubble from neighbouring fields flew up into the air. The wind seemed "confined" to a small area and seemed to move around them as if it had "a mind of its own", "doing funny things". After about a minute and a half, this wind moved away from them and vanished as soon as it had came. Although only Martin remembers watching the circle form, his whole family recall the unusual wind which almost knocked them off their feet, on an otherwise calm day.

So little did Martin think about what he had just witnessed, it didn't occur to him to go and look closer at the circle which had just arrived in front of his eyes. The experience had "felt strange" but hadn't shaken or frightened him, and he thought little more about the event until he recounted it to a work colleague some time later, who listened in amazement!

This event, and others like it which have been recorded elsewhere, show clearly that the crop circle phenomenon is something far beyond the mundane explanations that sceptics would have us accept. These witnessed occurrences don't of course reveal the identity (if any) of the 'hand' behind the invisible force (invisible apart from often-reported light phenomena) which lays the crops down but do demonstrate beyond doubt that something fascinating and defiantly unexplained is taking place in the fields around us.

At the end of 1991, the Centre for Crop Circle Studies, Sussex branch, was put together by a group of people determined to find at least some of the answers to the mystery of the crop designs. They would be ready by the next summer to tackle the beautiful field enigmas of 1992.

Three formations in one field at Patcham (91/04). Photo: Barry Reynolds.

Formation overlooking the new junction of the A23 and A27 at Patcham in 1992 (92/04). Photo: David Russell.

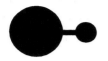

1992

Ref: 92/01
Location: Patcham, East Sussex
Map Ref: 306 960
Date: 24/6/92

Ref: 92/05
Location: Rye, East Sussex
Map Ref: 914 198
Date: End/6/92

Ref: 92/02
Location: Sompting, West Sussex
Map Ref: 157 610
Date: 24/6/92

Ref: 92/06
Location: Warnham, West Sussex
Map Ref: 169 335
Date: 7/7/92

Ref: 92/03
Location: West Blatchington, East Sussex
Map Ref: 280 082
Date: 27/6/92

Ref: 92/07
Location: Charlwood, West Sussex
Map Ref: 248 398
Date: End/6/92

Ref: 92/08
Location: Sompting, West Sussex
Map Ref: 166 044
Date: End/6/92

Ref: 92/09
Location: Steyning, West Sussex
Map Ref: 170 110
Date: Mid/7/92

Ref: 92/04
Location: Patcham, East Sussex
Map Ref: 300 095
Date: 29/6/92

Ref: 92/10
Location: Chilgrove, West Sussex
Map Ref: 833 129
Date: 20/7/92

1992

With the creation of the Centre for Crop Circle Studies, Sussex branch, at the end of 1991, this year's more diverse Sussex formations were the first to be fully documented and surveyed.

The Aftermath Defied

In the wake of the huge publicity given to the Doug and Dave scam in the autumn of 1991, one might reasonably have expected the circle phenomenon and those interested in it to have quietly vanished into obscurity. While the attention surrounding crop circles was certainly far less in 1992 nationally, the hard facts were that the formations were defiantly back once more, as if to prove that the two pranksters' "retirement" would not affect a phenomenon which had very little to do with them in the first place. In Sussex the interest in crop circles actually grew, with the birth in the late months of 1991 of the Sussex branch of the Centre for Crop Circle Studies (CCCS), an international organisation dedicated to studying the phenomenon. A letter sent out to all Sussex-based members of the national CCCS by Barry Reynolds, who had documented many of the previous years' Sussex formations, led to a gathering of about seventeen dedicated enthusiasts at the Burgess Hill Scout Centre, where CCCS Sussex meets to this day. At this meeting, an informal constitution was set up and guidelines as to how circle research should be carried out by the team the following summer were discussed. It was at this meeting that the idea for the monthly journal SC (or *Sussex Circular* as it was known then) was born. Little did we know that only two years later our group's numbers would be in the hundreds and that our local publication would be going out all over the world as one of the major sources of all crop circle information.

With this new investigative structure in place, the newly-born CCCS Sussex lay in wait for what might grace the fields in the coming months. We were not to be disappointed.

The A27 Effect

The first Sussex formation of 1992 (92/01) clearly wanted to be noticed and set a trend that would continue for the following three events, and indeed later years. It appeared at Patcham on the 24th June, in the same field that had been host to three formations the previous year. This time, it was further to the south of the field - right next to the newly built A27 Brighton by-pass, visible for all eastbound drivers to see. A moderately sized Sussex dumbbell shape in golden barley, it appeared virtually next

The first formation of 1992 (92/01) appeared at Patcham directly alongside the new stretch of the A27 the day it was officially opened. Photo: Andy Thomas.

to the spot where the opening ceremony of the new stretch of road took place - the very morning of the formation's appearance. Surely no coincidence. Perhaps the circle-making force was making some kind of statement as to what it thought of the new road. Certainly, it would appear to reiterate this 'statement' several times. Some believe that

crop circles appear where earth energy lines are disrupted by excavation as a way of balancing or releasing the broken energy flows.

The dumbbell contained two impressive centres, wound upright in knotted corn-dolly like tufts that were impossible to unthread. Both circles were laid clockwise. The large circle was 58' and the small 19', connected by a pathway 13' by 3'. The lay of the pathway was undirected and messier than the neater swirls of the circles, but as noted on other occasions, barley seems to be a harder medium for the circle-making force to deal with. Curiously, this part of the field was given over to the EC set-aside scheme from hereon and the pattern could still be seen in a green shape growing from fallen seedheads the following year. This often happens where fields with formations are harvested but not ploughed. 'New

Inside the Patcham dumbbell (92/01) the centres of the circles were twisted into incredible knots. Photo: Andy Thomas.

Age' travellers moved into the adjoining parkland in 1993 before being eventually moved on and barred by concrete blocks at the gateways. Were they attracted by the site's significance? Interestingly, Les Crawley, a local radio broadcaster for the BBC, witnessed a shining disc-shaped object hovering over this very field whilst out walking his dogs ten years previously. A very similar object was also spotted over the fields of nearby Pyecombe in the 1960s.

Perhaps the most impressive Sussex formation of 1992 appeared in very green wheat at Sompting, near Lambleys Lane (92/02). It began, according to the farmer, as a large simple circle on the same night that the Patcham dumbbell formed. The next night, 25th June, a more elaborate design arrived next to it; a ringed circle with two radiating arches, giving the impression of a spinning bow-tie or, as some remarked, the symbol worn by puppets from the television series *Captain Scarlet!* It was very large and was found in a field overlooking the A27 once again, only a few hundred yards west of the ancient church of St Mary's, off the Bostal Road which leads to Steyning. The single circle was 84' while the centre circle of the main design was 52', surrounded by a ring of 88'. The outer edges of the arches were 130' across. All the crop was laid clockwise, with the paths directed from the centre outwards. One of the paths of the arches pointed directly to the nearby church. The formation itself was barely visible from the A27, despite its proximity.

In another connection with road construction, this field was one of the ones scheduled to be cut through by the proposed A27 Worthing by-pass - a situation still

The pictogram at Sompting (92/02) was immaculate when it first appeared. One of the pathways appeared to point directly toward the church of St Mary's, which seems to be the centrepoint around which the formations in this area cluster. Photo: Andy Thomas.

pending. If it goes ahead, the same road will cut through the ancient sacred hillfort of Cissbury Ring, which many dowsers believe is the earth energy source for many of the crop formations in the Sompting area.

Walking through the maze of this design was an incredible experience and the apparent accuracy with which it had been constructed was breathtaking. Where the pathways formed the arches, crop had actually been bent at forty-five degrees to go around corners, curved at the nodal joints in some cases - an impossible effect to achieve by bending a stalk by hand. Later aerial shots, however, revealed that the shape of the formation was slightly stranger than expected, the proportions appearing odd. This worried some of the more sceptical researchers until the eminent American mathematician and scholar Professor Gerald Hawkins, author of the seminal work *Stonehenge Decoded*, which examined the unique geometry of the famous stone circle, contacted CCCS Sussex to congratulate us on having one of the first geometrically harmonious patterns of the year. The unusual proportions were seemingly deliberate, to enable it to conform mathematically.

The design was discovered to be very similar to old Knights Templar symbols, a medieval religious order often linked with occult practices and ancient ritual magic. One of these symbols was then actually found as a carving in the adjacent church of St Mary's - a church of great importance to the Knights Templars in the 12th century.

In an astounding example of synchronicity which was becoming familiar to croppies everywhere by this time, two days before the formation appeared, two brothers, Mark and Jason Porthouse, unwittingly made a joint request for a crop circle to appear in their area. Jason, without knowing Mark's whereabouts or intentions, stood at the eastern end of Cissbury Ring behind Sompting, and asked that one might be created. Little did he know that his brother was standing on the hill behind St Mary's church at virtually the same time, making the same request. Two days later, the formation had appeared and from then on, coincidentally or not, the area around Cissbury Ring and St Mary's church would be the focus for much crop circle activity in the coming years.

A few weeks later, aerial reconnaissance discovered a more roughly created but similar-looking design in fields to the south of the A27 at Sompting (92/08). Investigation on the ground never managed to pinpoint the location and it was not surveyed.

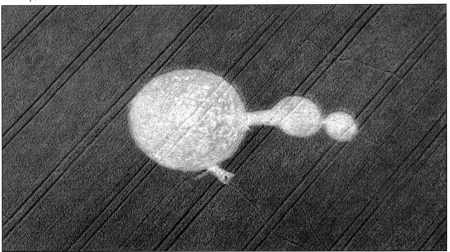

The pictogram at West Blatchington (92/03). The strange 'arm' emanating from the large circle appeared two days after the main formation. Photo: David Russell.

Whilst driving to Sompting to survey the Lambleys Lane formation, three members of the Sussex team spotted the third Sussex agriglyph of the year, yet again right next to the new stretch of the A27, at West Blatchington, about half a mile from the Patcham dumbbell, north-west of the turn-off to Devil's Dyke. Very visible to all drivers, this pattern (92/03) was made up of three circles, one perched offset upon the other, linked to a large circle by a short pathway. This appeared in wheat on 27th June. A small box or 'arm' emanating from the largest circle arrived later on the 29th June. The large circle was 72', the medium 29' and the smallest 20'. The pathway was 17' by 10'. All the circles again flowed clockwise.

A few days earlier, some researchers had spotted a thin flattened path of about 50' by 3' running down the side of this field which was heavily sloped to the south. No explanation was found, although some suggested an underground spring may have caused it by welling up and running through the crop. Later that week the formation appeared very close to the path. Perhaps, as some dowsers link the appearance of crop circles with the piezoelectric fields generated by running underground water, this path may have 'energised' the field to enable the design to be created. CCCS Sussex had to carry out the earliest survey of their careers at five in the morning in this formation as the farmer didn't want anyone to be seen inside as he felt it would encourage others into his field. Despite this, because of its high visibility, many drivers pulled up and hopped into the field in the subsequent weeks.

The design at the Patcham A23/A27 junction (92/04) was so perfectly formed it was as if a huge rubber stamp had pressed the shape into the field. Photo: Barry Reynolds.

Many of these same drivers might also have seen the next Sussex pattern to appear (92/04), back once again at Patcham, overlooking the new junction of the A23 and A27 in the field above the road construction caravans, only one field away from the first formation of the year and the same field as the dumbbell in 1991. This shape, which appeared in wheat on the 29th June, could be very clearly seen as one drove eastwards down the long hill of the A27 towards the junction. As with the 1991 Patcham events, there were reports that the workmen on the site heard strange sounds on the night the circles appeared, but this remains unconfirmed. The design was one large circle, linked in a triangle by paths with two smaller circles of differing size. Dubbed 'Mickey Mouse' by some researchers because of a very vague resemblance to the cartoon character (although this was truer of the Lewes pictogram of 1990), this was quite excellent in its quality, exquisitely laid down with very crisp edges and some of the most impressive centres yet seen in Sussex. The centre of the smallest circle was combed round like a fan, and the pathways spilled out into the flow of the circles like cascading water. (See pages 13 and 14.)

The large circle was 75', the medium circle 45' and the smallest 26', with all the circles again laid clockwise. Some researchers saw a link in the symbolism between all the formations which had appeared so far in 1992, particularly between this and 92/03 which appeared to be three similarly-proportioned circles and paths in a different combination.

A curious anecdote, which seems to suggest tricks being played with time, can be told of this Patcham event. On 28th June, the day before it appeared - or so it seemed - a friend of Barry Reynolds' parents spotted the formation in the morning and tried to contact them to report it, but they were out. However, both the CCCS Sussex team and Barry's parents had both driven past the field on several occasions that very day (on the way to and from surveying 92/02 at Sompting - the day 92/03 was discovered just a little way further up the A27 from Patcham) and had made a point of checking it, especially as it was a site of a formation the previous year. All - and one of these people was me - swear that the field was empty. And yet, a person holds fast to the fact that he had seen it in the field the day before! It would appear that either the Sussex team had momentarily become chronically unobservant (and yet managed to spot the new formation at West Blatchington) or a 'hole in time' carried the image of the pictogram forward a day for that one person - or he had a premonition that was so vivid, he believed he had actually witnessed it in reality! Of such legends, cerealogy is made.

After all the circle activity in the Patcham area this year and the last, many assumed that the circle-making force would be back here again the following year. In fact, no more patterns would appear again in this region until 1994 and the main 'centre of operations' was to shift to Sompting.

The Spread To The Borders

After such a concentration of formations in a relatively small area, the last Sussex agriglyphs of 1992 spread themselves out a little more as if to compensate, forcing members of the CCCS team (based mainly in central Sussex) to go as far as Rye for their next survey, right on the border with Kent. Only visible from a row of houses in the distance, this dumbbell pictogram in wheat (92/05) was very hard to find and lay in a flat field close to wet marshlands. Accompanying the dumbbell, which was in fact a ring connected by a long path to a slightly larger circle, was a single circle a few hundred feet away, in-between the tramlines with no visible signs of anyone having entered it. This circle, which was 17' across with a rather flattened edge on one side and had a lot of grass mixed in with the crop, was the first Sussex formation in 1992 to be laid anticlockwise. It was about a month old by the time it was discovered and probably appeared around the end of June. It was still in good condition when surveyed as few visitors had been in, probably due to the formation's virtual invisibility from the ground.

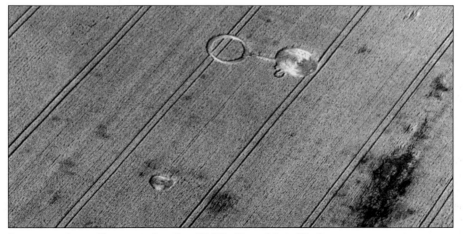

Pictogram and a neighbouring circle at Rye (92/05). Photo: Maria Ward.

The pathway in the main pictogram was set at a strange angle, meeting the circle more towards its edge instead of the middle, in enough of a way to suggest this was deliberate. Coming from the circle was a small 'loop', an elongated semi-circular ring just a few feet long, which appeared to point towards the single circle across the field. The centres of both the circles were even more offset from their logical places than is usual for crop circles (few circles have their centres at the mathematically correct spot - this offset effect has proved difficult to achieve in experiments with man-made circles). The circle of the dumbbell was 36', the ring 32', and the pathway 23' by 4'.

The phenomenon then moved to the north of the county around the 7th July, at Warnham, not far from the location of the first circle of 1990, on the by-pass linking Crawley to Horsham. Although this (92/06) was visible from the road, it was relatively small; tucked into the corner of a small triangular field bordered by trees, it could be easily missed. As a result, this formation was also little-visited. A simple circle of 34' with four small boxes attached at each 'corner', each about 5 by 2', it was on the messy side and the boxes were fairly indistinct but there was a good spiral swirl.

Back at the site of Doug and Dave's public misdemeanour the previous season, a new formation graced the fields of Chilgrove around 20th July, as if the circle-making force was reclaiming the area for itself. Like the pensioner's crude effort, this was again a dumbbell (92/10), but went one better in having one of the circles quadranted into quarters, with the crop swept in four different directions, similar to the Wiltshire event at Winterbourne Stoke in 1989 which marked a sudden acceleration of ingenuity by the phenomenon.

The last design reported during 1992 was at Charlwood, near Gatwick (92/07), in fields very close to the huge international airport. Although several passengers apparently spotted it when flying in on scheduled flights, news of the formation didn't reach CCCS Sussex until it had been harvested and no survey was carried out. Reports from one researcher who entered the field and studied the remaining floor pattern suggest it was of the 'triplet' variety, three circles in a line, linked by pathways.

Personal Circles

A year later, CCCS Sussex heard of one more, very small, formation which appeared (92/09). Karen Wolf, a lady from Steyning, was discussing crop circles with a friend and it was suggested that maybe she should 'ask' for a circle, as some had successfully done in the past (perhaps confirming the possible link with the human mind discussed earlier). Subsequent to this, one afternoon in July, Karen was walking with her young son in the local open space of Clay Field on the Clay Hill Road at Steyning, a privately owned meadow with a pond. Writing in SC (issue 21, Sep 93), Karen explains: "The owner lets the grass grow high and then harvests it for cattle. My son insisted on taking me into the field by a way I hadn't gone before and almost as soon as we got onto the land, there beneath my feet was a perfect circle about three or four feet across and also a bigger ring around, the circle not central within this ring... ...A few minutes after walking away from the circle, I was very much aware of a heaviness, like lead down the whole of my right side and I felt very peculiar... ...I've kicked myself a lot since then as I didn't go back and investigate further".

1993

Ref: 93/01
Location: Sompting, West Sussex
Map Ref: 167 047
Date: 7/6/93

Ref: 93/05
Location: Sompting, West Sussex
Map Ref: 145 070
Date: 28/6/93 & 17/7/93

Ref: 93/02
Location: Sompting, West Sussex
Map Ref: 167 056
Date: 23/6/93 & 2-5/7/93

Ref: 93/06
Location: Sompting, West Sussex
Map Ref: 166 063
Date: 29/6/93

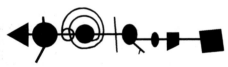

Ref: 93/03
Location: Sompting, West Sussex
Map Ref: 168 064
Date: 23, 29 & 30/6/93

Ref: 93/07
Location: Shoreham, West Sussex
Map Ref: 213 067
Date: 16/7/93

Ref: 93/08
Location: Felbridge, West Sussex
Map Ref: 367 382
Date: 10/8/93

Ref: 93/04
Location: Lancing, West Sussex
Map Ref: 205 064
Date: 25 & 27/6/93

1993

Sompting and Lancing became the major hotspot for Sussex formations, pictograms which grew were the order of the day, and strange objects were left lying around...

Mind Experiments

In May and June of 1993, CCCS Sussex mounted two experiments. One involved all the members concentrating on a chosen symbol (three circles joined by pathways in a triangular configuration) during meditations at the branch meetings to see if it were possible to influence the circle-making force to create a certain pattern. The other, an idea sparked by the main CCCS Chairman Michael Green and Sussex researcher Paul Bura, a psychic channeller (or 'medium'), consisted of attempts by a smaller group to set up a rendezvous point, by communicating with the circle-making force by psychic means, to enable a video recording of a crop circle being formed to be taken. High aims and strange concepts perhaps, but CCCS Sussex felt all approaches to the phenomenon should be tried in addition to the more conventional work being carried out.

It was with some excitement then that the first Sussex formation of 1993 (93/01) was discovered at Sompting in a field behind a housing estate on 7th June, the very night before a meeting held at Paul Bura's house the next day to discuss the forthcoming rendezvous experiment which was to take place later that month in a field at Devil's Dyke, near Brighton. The formation's appearance in this, the closest field to Paul's house in Lancing, seemed like a very good omen - and more to the point, its configuration bore a resemblance to the shape which CCCS Sussex members had meditated on the month before, except instead of three circles joined by paths, the formation was three circles around a larger circle, or a triangular triplet as it became known. Found in very young wheat, this was the earliest an event had been reported in Sussex so far. It was only lightly impressed in the crop, which grew back up again very

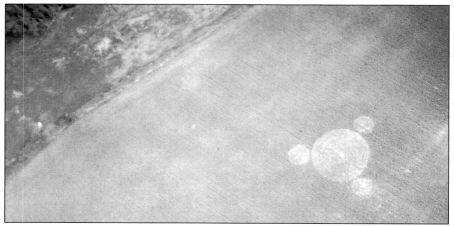

The faintness of the first 1993 formation, at Sompting (93/01), is due to the immaturity of the crop. The power cables from the pylon at the top left corner ran up to the fields where the first celtic cross and the 'sperm' formations were to appear. Note the lack of tractor tramlines in this field.
Photo: Michael Hubbard

quickly, as is often the case with circles in immature plants, but the lay and spiral of the crop was very neat. The main circle was 65' and the three circles surrounding it were each an average of 24'. All circles, in a break with the previous year's mainly clockwise direction, were laid anticlockwise. The crop itself was covered with a very fine layer of soil dust which seemed to have been thrown up by the force which created the circles. When touched or trodden on, this dust was immediately dislodged and any resulting markings on the crop were clearly visible. No such markings were found when the formation was first entered.

Very rarely for Sussex, this field had no tractor tramlines running through it and it was clear that no-one had originally entered the field, as walking through crop without leaving obvious trails is very difficult. However, later discovered in one of the smaller circles was an eight foot piece of orange baling twine with loops at both ends, as if a wooden pole had once gone through it. Sceptics immediately considered this proof of human pranksters at work until it was pointed out that the twine was entirely clean and that none of the powdery dust from the very dry soil (June was a very hot month in 1993), which the slightest movement threw up, was visible on it. This had clearly never been used in the construction of the formation but it had apparently been dropped inside it to give that impression. Other unlikely artefacts would be found as the summer progressed. Very close to the field was a row of houses lit by orange streetlights which illuminated the field well. A resident who spoke to CCCS Sussex said he was awake most of that night sitting by an open window which overlooks the field and he heard and saw nothing. Dr Levengood in the States was sent many samples from this formation and it was the first anywhere in the world to be sampled so extensively. In his opinion, the crop showed significant biological differences when compared to control samples taken from outside.

There were other neighbours nearby who had more of a mystical perspective on things. One lady (who first reported the formation) was a healer who had always wished for a pattern in this field; her son often had psychic visions of the field as it looked back in Saxon times. Another lady in the street had discovered a strange one-piece grey plastic motorcycle suit discarded by a nearby road a few days previously. On the night the triplet arrived, she dreamt of a "spaceman" who came to her house asking for the suit to be returned before walking off to a nearby spaceship. When she awoke next morning, the formation had appeared and its shape was very similar to that of the craft she had dreamt of.

Kebabs And Crosses

The second event of the year (93/02) was one of the most stunning yet. A 'celtic cross' design of a circle surrounded by four smaller satellite circles connected by a ring, appeared only about half a mile north from the triangular triplet and both fields actually had the same set of power cables running across them. This appeared in wheat on 23rd June at Sompting, next to the A27 on the north side of the road, about a quarter of a mile east of St Mary's church. Clearly Sompting was becoming a special site for circles. Many dowsers believed that earth energy was emanating from Cissbury Ring, coming down to St Mary's and being distributed out radially along energy lines to feed the formations which appeared in the vicinity, formations which would continue up to 1995. This celtic cross dowsed very strongly indeed.

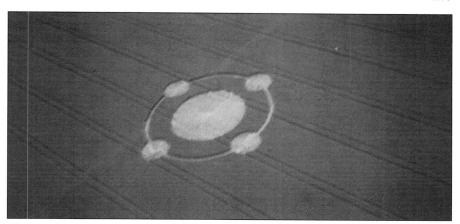

The first celtic cross at Sompting (93/02). The faint line crossing the field and the formation marks the site of an underground pipeline. Photo: Michael Hubbard

The pattern was very crisply imprinted and geometrically perfect to the nearest inch as later work on the survey data would prove. The lay of the crop was complex and included much multi-layering and bending of nodes, with even a radial flow at one point. Otherwise, everything was laid anticlockwise. The main circle was 57', the ring was 97' by 3' and each satellite measured an average of 22'. Some of the stems discovered inside seemed to have been completely blown apart from the inside as if they had been heated to the point of explosion. One stem even showed a small amount of soot-like substance.

On the night the formation appeared a nearby resident reported their alarm system going off at 1.15am and local animals were also disturbed. That same night, Paul Bura had inexplicable visions of a celtic cross pattern which he felt compelled to get up and draw on a piece of paper... he was told the next day, to his amazement, of the shape's appearance in a crop field.

In a trend-setting pattern that would be followed throughout the year, this design later grew a 'wedge' shape on the eastern-most satellite, connecting it to the main circle, and two pathways appeared from the ring to the central circle next to it. Other thin paths and an odd 'G' shape also appeared but these were more dubious. Quite visible from the A27, the field had a public footpath running through it and the formation was much visited. Not far from this footpath, a broken wooden pole with baling twine and what appeared to be sea-fishing swivels attached was found in a tramline. The twine matched that found in the triangular triplet and the pole fitted into the looped twine found there. There now seemed little doubt that someone was trying to make the Sompting crop circles look as if they had been man-made by leaving potential hoaxing implements around. In both cases, however, neither the twine nor the pole were dirty in any way that one might expect from something used to crush down dusty crop, and the unlikelihood that the same hoaxers could be so careless as to leave their tools behind twice rather deflated the intended effect. Who could have been responsible? A consortium of local hostile farmers eager to put off people's interest? A sceptical croppie eager to be proved right? Something more sinister? Maybe the truth will never be known.

Three stages of a growing formation at Sompting (93/03): Beginning as a single circle, little more than a smudge in a field (with the 'intestines' pathways to the right), it subsequently grew a line of strange shapes, mutating again to culminate in its final bizarre configuration. Photos: Barry Reynolds.

On the same night the celtic cross arrived, within viewing distance from that field, a single circle with two thin paths was found in a wheat field about a quarter of a mile north at Steepdown Titchill (93/03). This circle, as predicted by dowser David Russell, was to grow extensively over the next few weeks. On the 29th June, six further shapes appeared next to the circle in a long line, connected by very long thin pathways. Each shape was different; a ring, a circle, two egg-shapes, and two odd rectangular 'blocks'. Its unusual random look gave rise to the nickname 'the kebab'. Because of its strange shape many researchers disliked the formation but the lay of the crop, especially in the square-edged blocks, was extremely good and significantly bent nodes were found inside. The different shapes averaged a size of 10' to 15' and the overall length of the pictogram was 152'. All the separate elements flowed anticlockwise except the second egg shape which was clockwise.

On 30th June, the kebab grew yet again, this time with the addition of a large double spiral from the second circle, two different length arms, one from the first egg and another on the pathway, and an arrowhead at the front pointing southwards, giving quite a bizarre appearance overall and taking the length to 172'. These final additions were messier than the original parts of the formation. 50' or so from it, a network of random squiggly lines, nicknamed 'the intestines' (!) were found and at first were taken to be animal tracks but seemed to display qualities of crop circle pathways when examined closer. One researcher claimed the additions to the kebab appeared in response to experiments he carried out with musical tones played in the formation but later analysis cast doubt on the correlation of the dates given. A team led by the Hampshire-based cerealogist Lucy Pringle used this formation to carry out tests with brain-wave monitoring equipment to view human responses to crop circles, before being thrown out of the field by an angry friend of the farmer who refused to believe they had permission to be there when in fact they did!

On 25th June, in a wheat field about a mile east of Sompting below the huge A27 Lancing flyover junction, another cross shape appeared (93/04), although not of the celtic variety. This was a small circle with four long arms each culminating in even smaller circles. It was on fairly marshy land, very close to the River Adur, under the gaze of the famous Lancing College Chapel and directly under the approach flightpath for Shoreham airport on the opposite side of the road. It could be seen clearly from the flyover when heading east. Only two days later, on 27th June and before anyone could survey it in its original form, the central circle expanded to cover the arms of the cross, leaving a formation which bore a close resemblance to the Warnham event of 1992 (92/06) in shape and quality, a circle with four circles at each 'corner' which was interestingly but indistinctly laid. Despite its messy appearance, the way the crop flowed was very detailed and complex. The swirl of the circle was made up with bands of counter-rotating directions, some clockwise, others anticlockwise, with crop bending at the nodes in some places where the crop changed its direction mid-way. It was as if several adjoining rings had been added to the original circle. The paths of the original arms could still be seen lying underneath the newly laid crop. The overall size of the subsequent main circle was 93', and the average size of the small circles was 6'.

On the night the cross mutated, CCCS Sussex were out conducting their first rendezvous experiment a few miles away. (No firm results were achieved but two more attempts were made over the summer, one of them sited inside the kebab formation.) Although speculation, some believe the growth of the Lancing cross occurred as a muted response to the experiment carried out that night. Work with electrostatic meters produced some interesting anomalies in the expected amount of electrostatic voltage contained within the area of the crop circle compared with that of the rest of the field.

A week after the first celtic cross was discovered, an almost identical one arrived half a mile west of St Mary's church at Sompting on 28th June, looking quite magnificent. This time the pattern (93/05) was in golden barley on the side of a hill opposite a derelict farmhouse, which gave very good viewing from the new trading estate north of the A27 on the border of Sompting and Worthing. Very slightly larger than its brother, the main circle was 62' with an average of 23' for the satellites. The ring was 97' by 3'. All was laid anticlockwise. Several weeks later, on 17th July, a grapeshot circle appeared next to one of the satellite circles. In this formation, four painted silver pebbles were found in the centre of the main circle, placed in the configuration of the triangular triplet. Whether these were put there, as with the other objects found this summer, to spread mischief or were simply an offering or ritual meditational aid placed there by a mystical devotee was never discovered. No more strange objects, suspicious or otherwise were found in any Sussex crop formations after. During the meditation experiment on the chosen design earlier in the year, CCCS Sussex member Paula Mitton had a vision of where the shape might turn up. She wrote it down, and sent her description, privately, to SC in May, should it turn out to be significant. Although the shape itself did not appear, the location she gave was uncannily close to that of this celtic cross, including a description of the old derelict farmhouse opposite.

The Sperm

Standing in the kebab pictogram looking west, the lower part of the field which contained the first celtic cross lay opposite although the cross itself was over the brow of the hill. Next to the power cables crossing the field (the same ones which ran from the triangular triplet), what looked like simply a strange path in the field appeared on 29th June and turned out to be an actual formation which could easily have been missed. It earned itself the name 'the sperm' (93/06); a small oval ring with a long bent tail. Inside the oval, which was approximately 17' by 3', the crop was laid anticlockwise and a single stem stood upright and unaffected in the middle of the flattened ring. The tail trailed off from the ring for about 87' before abruptly changing direction back on itself for another 87'. The nature of the path was reminiscent of the 'intestines' found next to the kebab on the hill opposite. In a curious 'coincidence', when CCCS Sussex branch convenor Barry Reynolds first charted the map reference for the nearby celtic cross (as 166 063 instead of 167 056), he got it wrong by several hundred feet before correcting the mistake. Incredibly, this reference turned out to be the exact co-ordinates of where the 'sperm' finally appeared!

Snails And Cycles

With the A27 clearly still an attractive location for the phenomenon, the next formation to appear (93/07) on 16th July in wheat, was very close to the site of the Mill Hill circles of 1990, in the same field, north of Shoreham just before the flyover where the expanding cross appeared earlier in the year. Quickly dubbed 'the snail', it recalled the appearance of some of the 'insectograms' which had appeared in Wiltshire in 1991, with a dumbbell body of a double-ringed circle at one end and a smaller circle with one protruding 'antenna' at the other. Orbiting the formation were a triangle and two rectangular boxes, one shorter than the other. Two tiny grapeshot circles were also found several hundred feet from the main shapes. Some thin, scrappy additions which arrived in the weeks after resembled those of the later first celtic cross mutations and were probably inflicted by the same, probably human, perpetrator. Due to a misunderstanding with the farmer, who had asked CCCS Sussex to wait until just before harvest before surveying the formation, it was cut down early and the surveys were carried out on the visible floor pattern that remained. The ringed circle was 64', the small circle 24', and the triangle 18' by 19' by 23'. All swirls were anticlockwise. Compass readings revealed that the designs had been positioned in such an accurate way that two lines running direct north-south could be drawn, one touching the edge of the small circle, going through the centre of the long box and touching a point of the triangle, the other touching the edge of the large ringed circle and a corner point of the small box.

A very good view of the formation could be had from standing on the bridge over the A27 to Mill Hill, facing east. Just a little further up from this, above the field heading north-west, is a gravel car-park for sightseers wishing to look out at the beautiful view across the Adur valley. On the night the snail appeared, Jason Porthouse, who with his brother Mark had simultaneously asked for a crop formation in Sompting shortly before the 1992 pictogram appeared, pulled his motorcycle into this area at about midnight. In the darkness, he meditated for a while, asking for some kind of positive proof from the circle-making force of its existence. After a while, he left for home. The next morning the pictogram had appeared in the adjacent field.

After all the circle activity having been centred exclusively on the Sompting/Lancing area, it was something of a surprise that the last Sussex event of 1993 (93/08) was up at Felbridge, East Grinstead. Hidden away in a large but isolated field, close to the Worth Way footpath, this formation, once again in wheat, was found on 10th August and appeared on the front cover of the *East Grinstead Courier* in a full colour photograph, with the farmer standing at the centre. A double-ringed circle with two crossbars, a long path of two angles emanated from it, ending in a small circle with three thin pathways radiating, giving the initial appearance of a circus monocycle although more mystical-minded researchers claimed it represented a dragon! The lines of the crossbars were on the exact points of the compass. Discovered in the centre of the middle circle was a circular blackened patch about a foot wide which didn't seem to have resulted from burning. Unfortunately, there was no time to investigate this further as the field was being harvested when the research team arrived to survey it, although the farm workers agreed to delay their work while measurements were taken. In a change from most of the other designs of the year - opposite to 1992 - the crop was laid clockwise. The outer ring was 68' by 6', the long pathway including the change of angle was 50' by 2', the small circle was 7' and the radiating pathways were 11' on average.

The appearance of a formation on the outskirts of the county after a proliferation down on the central coast seemed to mirror the events of 1992, except that in 1993 it was Sompting, not Patcham, which played host to most of the Sussex agriglyphs. Sompting wasn't going to be ignored in 1994 either...

1994

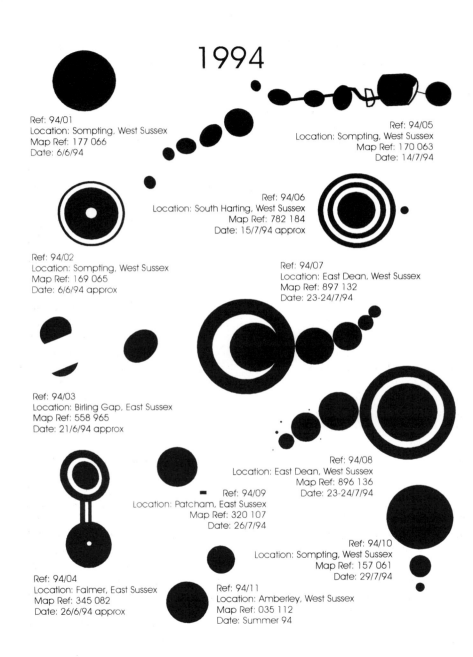

Ref: 94/01
Location: Sompting, West Sussex
Map Ref: 177 066
Date: 6/6/94

Ref: 94/05
Location: Sompting, West Sussex
Map Ref: 170 063
Date: 14/7/94

Ref: 94/06
Location: South Harting, West Sussex
Map Ref: 782 184
Date: 15/7/94 approx

Ref: 94/02
Location: Sompting, West Sussex
Map Ref: 169 065
Date: 6/6/94 approx

Ref: 94/07
Location: East Dean, West Sussex
Map Ref: 897 132
Date: 23-24/7/94

Ref: 94/03
Location: Birling Gap, East Sussex
Map Ref: 558 965
Date: 21/6/94 approx

Ref: 94/08
Location: East Dean, West Sussex
Map Ref: 896 136
Date: 23-24/7/94

Ref: 94/09
Location: Patcham, East Sussex
Map Ref: 320 107
Date: 26/7/94

Ref: 94/10
Location: Sompting, West Sussex
Map Ref: 157 061
Date: 29/7/94

Ref: 94/04
Location: Falmer, East Sussex
Map Ref: 345 082
Date: 26/6/94 approx

Ref: 94/11
Location: Amberley, West Sussex
Map Ref: 035 112
Date: Summer 94

1994

Sompting continued to be active, another area of Sussex received some of the best formations yet witnessed in the county, and some very unusual effects were discovered at Birling Gap...

A Different Feel

1994 immediately felt like a new 'approach' was being taken by the circle-making force. Whilst the fields of Wessex became alive with some of the most staggering formations yet witnessed, Sussex was treated to a quieter start to the summer compared to the previous year.

The season began very simply, on 6th June, at Sompting yet again, in a field of wheat above the approach road to Worthing refuse tip, exactly one day less than a year from the triangular triplet of 1993, thus taking the crown as the earliest Sussex event. A single circle (94/01) about 75' across, it was reported by three different researchers out looking for formations independently on the same day a week or so after it appeared; a curiosity bearing in mind it was not highly visible from any main roads, although good viewing could be had from the tip access road. It was as if these three people (one of whom was me) had simultaneously been given the go-ahead that the circle season had begun and that they should go out searching in the same place!

The circle was very lightly impressed, as if it had only been brushed by whatever lays the crops down. It was virtually invisible when actually standing within it, as by the time the circle was surveyed all the crop was standing up almost as normal. Even allowing for the fact that young crop often grows up again, this suggests the plants were never laid very flat. This also would seem to put paid to one rumour that "forty hunt saboteurs" made the formation - forty people in one spot would have crushed the crop down irreparably. When viewed from a distance, a spiral-effect could be discerned within the edges of the circle, as if the crop had originally been laid down not as a flattened circle but as a path spinning inwards, anticlockwise.

Interestingly, the ridge at the top of this field is a continuation of The Ridgeway, an ancient path which crosses southern England all the way from Wiltshire, site of so many crop designs, to Lancing Ring, site of an old Roman Villa.

Directly opposite the field, on the other side of the tip access road, is another field which curves over the brow of a hill and was host to the first Sompting pictogram in 1990, adjoining the field where the kebab formation had been in 1993. On the same day the single circle was discovered, also found was the second formation of 1994 (94/02) in this field of wheat. It was extremely small and looked very insignificant from the nearby Bostal Road at Sompting Abbotts looking east; investigation revealed it to be a tiny but beautiful ringed circle, laid anticlockwise with a standing tuft of crop at its centre. A tightly-swirled fan of wheat ringed this standing clump which must have been exquisite when it first appeared. It had obviously been there a while when discovered (15th June) and probably formed about the same time as its neighbour, as the farmer reported having spotted the formation when crop spraying two weeks previously - it had already been driven over when surveyed, as it was positioned directly on the tractor tramlines. The circle was 15' and the ring 20'.

The Birling Gap Surprise

Although continuing the trend of seemingly simpler patterns for 1994, the Sussex season suddenly produced a surprise which was to cause ripples throughout circle research across the world. At Birling Gap, near the coastal beauty spot of Beachy Head, Eastbourne, on June 21st, a small oval shape (94/03) was spotted in a barley field from the road which leads to the sea, overlooked by the old Belle Tout lighthouse. CCCS Sussex decided to investigate further, and was glad when it did. Inside the egg-shaped formation it was easy to see why it looked indistinct from the road; instead of the expected swirl of flattened crop, all the crop was bent over *halfway up the stems*, the heads of the plants being woven together with the ones next to them in clumps, knotted so tightly it was impossible to separate them. This was truly astonishing. The oval was made up of a web of suspended crop about a foot high, the tops of the plants all laid out in an extraordinary weave. It was impossible to walk inside without leaving huge footprints in the crop.

Further up the field, going east, another very similar formation was discovered, exhibiting the same incredible effect except that this oval shape appeared to have a flat edge to it, as if part of its shape had been removed - which is exactly what had happened. Power lines crossed the field on telegraph poles and ran directly above the cut-off point. Over the other side of the cables was the missing part of the formation - a thinner oval with a flat edge facing its counterpart. The two edges were exactly the same measurement - 27'. (The first oval was 25' by 30', and the flat-edged oval was 27' by 33'.)

Following the power lines to the end of the field revealed the same halfway-bent effect in long strips along the wire fence at the end, culminating in a triangular area in the corner of the field where the fence met a stone wall. These strips and the shape which appeared to have been sliced in half, gave rise to the theory that a descending circle-making energy had come from above, formed one oval without trouble, but then hit the cables with the second, literally cutting itself in half to result in the bisected formation. The rest of the energy then rushed along the power cables to the lightning conductor, which ran down to the wire fence, and then dispersed itself along the back of the field.

Some sceptical researchers proposed a more mundane explanation for the amazing effects discovered in these formations - birds, specifically rooks. Birds have been known to cause circular patches of damage in dry summers while trying to nibble moisture out of growing crops, and have been known to roughly bend crop halfway down. However, this explanation for the Birling Gap events does not explain the very complex weaving which resulted in barley heads so twisted together that they couldn't be pulled apart. It also doesn't explain the very crisp, clear oval shapes, nor the incredible coincidence of the two flat edges of the sliced formation fitting exactly. The farm manager for these fields accompanied the survey team into the field and stated categorically that no bird could have caused damage of the nature seen in these formations, as he was familiar with rook destruction. In some of the wilder areas around the fences and telegraph poles, stray plants from other surrounding fields were growing and were also affected by the same phenomena, including oilseed rape, which is virtually impossible to bend halfway up a stem without breakage occurring. It is also interesting to note that Dr Levengood in the States discovered some of the highest

From the road, the Birling Gap formations (94/03 – just one of the shapes is visible here) were unremarkable – inside was quite another story. The 'Belle Tout' lighthouse can be seen in the distance. Photo: Andy Thomas.

Inside the Birling Gap formations (94/03), an astonishing effect was discovered – all the crop had been bent over halfway up the stems!
Photo: Barry Reynolds.

The heads of the bent plants at Birling Gap (94/03) were woven tightly together in little 'nests' like this one. Photo: Barry Reynolds.

recorded biological differences yet found between the circle-affected crop from these formations and control samples.

Clearly, the Birling Gap events were very significant, and virtually unique, although less well-documented similar-type occurrences have since been reported in other parts of the world - notably in sweetcorn in the USA (a difficult challenge for rooks!). News of their appearance spread rapidly throughout the croppie world and several international researchers, including Colin Andrews and CCCS Chairman Michael Green, came to Sussex especially to witness them. What excited many was that here, at last, were circles that no hoaxer could possibly claim to have made as it was impossible to walk in them without leaving very obvious footprints - although that didn't stop one researcher flailing at an experimental patch of crop with a stick to see if the effect could be convincingly replicated... The Birling Gap formations, so seemingly insignificant at first, turned out to be the talking point of the whole summer for some, generating debate which continues to this day.

The Rough With The Smooth

The next pattern to be discovered (94/04) displayed a similar effect to that seen at Birling Gap in one very small part of it at least - a small standing tuft in an unusual dumbbell in barley at Falmer to the east of the University of Brighton buildings behind the Moulsecoomb estate, was bent over halfway up the stems in the same manner. The rest was laid more conventionally, although this was not easy to realise as by the time the formation was surveyed after being spotted by aerial surveillance on 26th June it had been there for some time and was extremely trampled and weather-worn. In fact this was the type of event that the casual observer could easily dismiss as being nothing more than the work of local children from the nearby houses - certainly, the whole lower part of the field which borders a footpath from the estate was criss-crossed with rough paths where dogs had run and youths had obviously played. In fact, close inspection revealed very interesting lays of the crop, not least the bent stems in the standing tuft which was at the centre of a circle which connected to a ringed oval at a strange angle by way of two straight paths. Dr Levengood examined samples from the dumbbell and was happy that it displayed significant changes from unaffected crop.

Although not visible from the ground in the field itself, the formation could be seen clearly, if briefly, from the new stretch of the A27 coming east down towards the Southern Water offices with Coldean to the right, although it was not impressive and relatively small. The circle was 26' and the oval ring was 29' by 31', width approximately 7'. The overall length of the dumbbell was 67'.

Another design to appear, in wheat on July 14th, wasn't to break the mould of the strange but fascinating glyphs which had so far deigned to arrive in Sussex in 1994. With the appearance of what became rapidly known as 'kebab II' (94/05), Sussex researchers were beginning to think the geometrically beautiful celtic crosses and pictograms were things of the past, replaced instead by extremely odd but exquisitely constructed curios. They needn't have worried. But for now, the new kebab, like its predecessor, had arrived at Sompting once more, 400' to the south of the tiny ringed circle (94/02) in the same field. A good view could be had from the top of the Bostal Road. Once more, here was a long string of strange ovals and block-like shapes arranged in a line, with perhaps more flow and roundness than the previous kebab only one field west the year before. It also displayed the same capacity to grow extra bits as the weeks went on. Starting with five different shapes, with one oval on its own 100' or so east from the main formation, it gradually grew until at the last count there were thirteen (!) different shapes all laid out in a rather long bent line.

Despite its odd look, the inside was laid with some of the most beautiful flows and gorgeously swirled centres yet seen in any of the Sussex fields. The middles of the small ovals in particular were laid down in incredible fans of anticlockwise spiralled wheat, very finely formed. Several stalks were found bent at the nodes more than once, swept around corners. Even more interestingly, in the separate oval at the top of the formation, a fine, silvery dust was found covering a small expanse of the laid crop, rather like metallic paint had been sprayed. On these same stalks, several tiny bright red dots were found which didn't seem to correspond to any known plant disease. Samples of these plants were sent away for analysis but no firm results were forthcoming.

The lay of the crop in 'kebab II' at Sompting (94/05) was exquisite. Photo: Andy Thomas.

Most of the shapes were about 15' by 20' except the lower block which was 31'. The total length of the original configuration was 130', growing much longer with the many additions (which were harvested before they could be surveyed), although one of the final shapes looked like someone's attempt to write their initials into the crop and didn't resemble the other new parts.

A New Area

After such a concentration of activity in the Sompting area, a new territory for the circles began quietly (or continued, from the tasters of Tangmere in 1943 and Chilgrove in 1992) with the appearance of a small double-ringed circle with a single grapeshot (94/06) at South Harting, very near the Hampshire border just below Petersfield. Appearing in wheat around 15th July, like several of the 1994 events it ran extremely close to the footpath of the famous South Downs Way which straddles the downland across much of Sussex. The formation was tucked into the corner of a field near a small reservoir, well hidden from any roads, and was consequently little visited. The lay of the crop was very neat and the central swirl had a lovely flow to it. Within the lay, small shards of shattered white plastic were found, as if a plastic cup or some other piece of litter had blown into the field and been pulverised by the circle-making force.

This lovely double-ringer at South Harting (94/06) began a new spate of formations in the western part of West Sussex. Photo: Steve Alexander

The central circle was 25', the rings and the gaps between them were exactly 3ft, and the grapeshot was 4', at a distance of exactly 4' from the formation. Everything was laid clockwise except for the grapeshot which flowed in the opposite direction. Little could anyone guess that this sweet little design was the precursor to two of the biggest and most impressive agriglyphs yet witnessed in Sussex, which would appear only a few miles away a week later.

Classic Formations At East Dean

Although all the formations which had visited the county so far in 1994 had been of huge interest to researchers, especially the Birling Gap events, there was still a lingering disappointment that nothing immediately visually arresting had been found. As if to finally reward patience, two extremely beautiful and huge crop patterns arrived at East Dean, near Singleton, above Chichester, between the 23rd and 24th July. Ironically, their relatively long distance from the heart of CCCS Sussex (based more in mid-Sussex) meant that many of the less mobile or tight-scheduled researchers never managed to visit the patterns for themselves. Maybe this was a message, that people shouldn't expect everything on a plate just where it suited them all the time... It was time for those in another region to be given a chance.

The first of the two East Dean beauties to be discovered (94/07) was the lower of the two, in a wheat field which overlooked the road that runs from Charlton, fairly close to the village church. A formation of huge dimensions, it appeared to fit into the sequence of what had become known as 'scorpion' or 'thought bubble' designs, which had been appearing elsewhere in the country in 1994, so called because of their tails of circles graduating from large to small. This version was a flattened circle of 185' (!) with a standing crescent moon shape inside it, followed by four more circles of 68', 50', 24' and 20', curving round to the right as they went. All the circles were laid anticlockwise - except the third tail circle, which was clockwise.

As the thought bubble patterns had begun to appear during the much-publicised collisions of the fragments of comet Shoemaker-Levy 9 into the planet Jupiter, many

One of the photographs of the Alfriston 1984 formation (84/01) which helped launch the crop circles into public awareness, as taken by the then Labour MP Denis Healey. The rough pathways were probably made by subsequent human sightseers. Photo: Denis Healey.

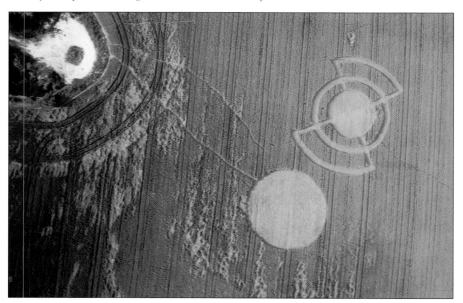

Pictogram and circle at Sompting in 1992 (92/02). Mathematician Professor Gerald Hawkins found many geometrical harmonies in this formation, explaining the rather odd proportions of the 'arches'. Photo: Michael Hubbard.

Inside the first celtic cross at Sompting in 1993 (93/02); the quality of the formation was breathtakingly beautiful. Photo: Barry Reynolds.

One of the striking 'thought bubble' formations at East Dean, near Chichester, 1994 (94/07), which attracted huge attention. Photo: Steve Alexander.

Researchers investigate rings in oilseed rape at Southsease, 1995 (95/01). Photo: Steve Alexander.

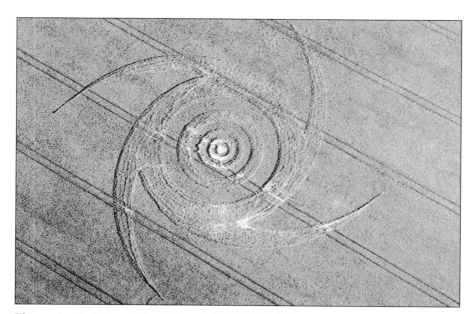

The stunning 'Catherine wheel' at Alfriston in 1995 (95/02). The crop was very young at this stage hence the faintness of the design. Photo: Michael Hubbard.

The 'time tunnel' at Cissbury Ring, 1995 (95/10), one of the finest formations ever seen in Sussex. The accuracy of the off-centre geometry is astonishing. Photo: Michael Hubbard.

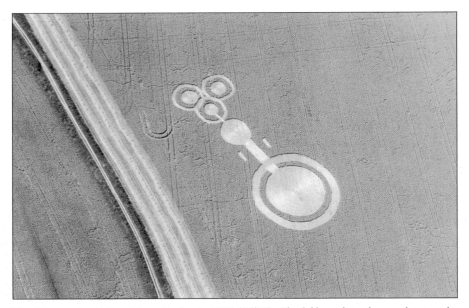

The elaborate dumbbell at Upper Beeding in 1995 (95/12). The field was being harvested just as this picture was taken, only one day after its appearance. The farmer was keen to get rid of the formation, to deter sightseers. Photo: Jason Porthouse.

speculated that these long tails of circles might represent the fragments crashing into the gas giant. It was fascinating to see that one of the photographs taken of the black scars from the collisions showed a shape almost identical to the East Dean formation, hundreds of miles across on the surface of Jupiter...

For some, this remains the most stunning Sussex agriglyph to date, and many witnessed the formation because of the local television news coverage accorded to it - which did not amuse the farmer. His wife eventually took to guarding the field at weekends in a camper van to prevent sightseers entering the field. One of the most upsetting things for the farmer was that the pattern had appeared in a field which was intended as seed crop for another generation of wheat, and not for standard harvest. The arrival caused consternation in the local community, who were at first caught up in the novelty of being in the limelight, but quickly came to resent it. Ancient folklore runs deep in close-knit country communities even today, and fears of the formation being a bad omen were voiced by some, especially those of the Christian persuasion, one of whom referred to it as "a product of dangerous thinking"! Unfounded rumours of the pattern being a hoax were quickly circulated perhaps in an attempt to defuse the strong feelings this enigmatic appearance had generated. One such rumour was born of a man being spotted coming out of the field with a long metal pole early one morning - in fact this turned out to be a well-known crop circle photographer carrying his equipment for overhead shots...

A number of curious 'coincidences' surrounded this formation. On the night it appeared, locals reported many disturbances amongst farm animals in the area, in particular, there was a commotion amongst geese and cows in the early hours of the morning. Such disturbances have often been reported in association with the circle phenomenon throughout the country; some put this down to animals picking up the high-pitched whistling sounds some eye-witnesses to crop circles forming have reported. The crescent moon shape embodied in the large circle was by now a common recurrence in English formations - but was it coincidence that the woods which bordered the field to the north were known as 'Half Moon Piece'? Most interestingly of all, Jenni Cassel, an artist from Binsted who had recently started incorporating crop circle designs into her paintings (from photographs; she had never witnessed one for herself), decided to paint a picture of East Dean by night a few days before the glyph was found. In her painted sky was the moon, overlooking the village...

Unknown to most, just over the brow of the hill from the half-moon design (at a place known as Greenhill, site of an ancient settlement), an only slightly less large and similar formation (94/08) had arrived on the same night in a field of barley. The major difference was that instead of a flattened circle with a standing crescent, this was a large ringed circle with a total diameter of 128', with a tail of three circles, 62', 38' and 21'. Five tiny grapeshot circles, varying from 2' to 4', two of which appeared several days later, were scattered around the lower tail circles. All the crop was laid anticlockwise.

This was far less accessible and almost invisible from ground level. Some reports say one of the East Dean shapes was visible from nearby Goodwood Racecourse. If true, it's likely that it was this formation as opposed to the lower one, which was in a valley. This configuration, though of excellent proportions, was rougher inside than its very finely laid near-twin, probably due to the fact that it was barley, not wheat. Its virtual invisibility at close quarters meant that it was hardly visited at all - which must have been a great relief for the farmer. The moon-shape in the lower formation and the ringed circle in the Greenhill one led some to speculate that the two represented lunar and solar symbols.

At the end of the season, after harvest, researchers learnt of one more event in this general area (94/11) at Camp Hill, near Amberley. All that is known is that two circles of differing size were spotted in the same field, in an unspecified crop, again very close to the South Downs Way.

First Rape Formation

On July 26th, a first for Sussex occurred back at an old haunt, between Patcham and Ditchling Beacon - a circle in oilseed rape. Formations in this distinctive bright yellow crop are much sought by researchers because rape is a plant which is notoriously difficult to tread down without leaving very visible and extensive damage. 1994 had begun with a spate of rape events in the Avebury area of Wiltshire and it was hoped that Sussex would follow suit, but to no avail. However, as if to quell the disappointment, we were thrown a last-minute titbit as a taster for the gratification that would come in 1995.

From the road that runs between the A27 and the beauty spot of Ditchling Beacon, a single circle (94/09) was discovered in the distance, looking west. By this time of the year the gorgeous yellow bloom had completely vanished and the field of rape was green. As far as could be ascertained, this was the first recorded instance of a rape formation appearing after the flowers had died. 23' in diameter, and spiralled clockwise, the lay of the swirl was very neat and the extremely long stems (rape can grow to about 5' in

Inside the rape circle between Ditchling Beacon and Patcham (94/09). By the time this formation appeared, the distinctive yellow flowers had already died down. Photo: Danny Sotham.

height), by now very sticky with their oily substances, were curved accordingly. As noted before, centres of circles are often very offset from their expected positions - this centre was offset about 3' to the south. With the wall of surrounding high stems, the circle had a very atmospheric, secluded feel about it. About 40' to the east was a rectangular marking, about 4' by 3' (a rectangular grapeshot?). In a nearby bush, a child's silver helium balloon had lodged in the hedgerow from somewhere, and was not a UFO, should anyone have spotted it...

A Final Thought...

The Sussex season of 1994 ended where it began, back at Sompting - in the same field and on exactly the same spot as the 1992 (92/02) pictogram. On 31st July, another in the series of 'thought bubble' designs was discovered in wheat at Lambleys Lane (94/10), only this time it was much smaller than its brothers at East Dean, with one large circle of 90', and two tail circles of 27' and 14', all spiralled anticlockwise. It's interesting to note that the further out from Wiltshire this series of designs got, the shorter the tails of circles became, this one probably being the furthest of its ilk. Curiously, a line drawn through the centres of each circle in this formation revealed all three to be aligned exactly magnetic north to south.

This year, the crop in the field was very thin and scrappy, with a high proportion of grass and weeds growing amongst the wheat, which had been swept into the swirls of the circles in the same manner as the laid crop, which was not very flat. This was interesting, but it did give them an untidy look. Later work on the geometric qualities of these circles revealed some impressive correlations between the ratios of their respective sizes and the configuration in which they were placed.

With this formation the season closed, leaving Sussex croppies to look back on an unusual but important series of formations with a new geographical spread. 1995 was to provide an equally challenging and important series of landscape enigmas...

The lesser-seen of the two impressive formations at East Dean (94/08). Photo: Steve Alexander.

Ref: 95/06
Location: Binsted, West Sussex
Map Ref: 993 051
Date: 1/7/95

1995

Ref: 95/07
Location: Saltdean, West Sussex
Map Ref: 388 028
Date: 2/7/95

Ref: 95/01
Location: Southease, East Sussex
Map Ref: 421 049
Date: 8/5/95

Ref: 95/08
Location: Denton, East Sussex
Map Ref: 458 016
Date: 9/7/95

Ref: 95/09
Location: Shoreham, West Sussex
Map Ref: 214 068
Date: 8/7/95 approx

Ref: 95/02
Location: Alfriston, East Sussex
Map Ref: 527 033
Date: 31/5/95

Ref: 95/10
Location: Cissbury Ring, West Sussex
Map Ref: 155 087
Date: 15/7/95

Ref: 95/03
Location: Alfriston, East Sussex
Map Ref: 509 036
Date: 23/6/95

Ref: 95/11
Location: Cocking, West Sussex
Map Ref: 880 180
Date: 16/7/95 (man-made..?)

Ref: 95/12
Location: Upper Beeding, West Sussex
Map Ref: 199 096
Date: 23/7/95

Ref: 95/04
Location: Felbridge, West Sussex
Map Ref: 367 383
Date: 29/6/95

Ref: 95/13
Location: Compton, West Sussex
Map Ref: 776 147
Date: Summer 95

Ref: 95/05
Location: Kingley Vale, West Sussex
Map Ref: 824 110
Date: 22/6/95

Ref: 95/14
Location: Wilmington, East Sussex
Map Ref: 540 037
Date: 25/7/95

1995

The year that saw Sussex, by default, overtake Wiltshire in numbers of formations, a year of great variety for both the designs of the formations and the crops they appeared in.

A Geographical Challenge

1995 saw Sussex throw down a challenge, in terms of the numbers of formations which appeared, to the more usual regions of mass circle-activity, if only because other areas mysteriously had less agriglyphs than usual while Sussex remained consistent. The ancestral seat of Wiltshire as the centre of the crop circle universe saw its crown being given to Hampshire instead, and Sussex was next in line to the throne, having a total of fourteen separate formations. For the first time in years, Wiltshire was mysteriously shunned by the phenomenon, with only a few events, for reasons which remain unclear. Perhaps once again, the circle making force was trying to shake croppies from their complacency of expectations as to where the phenomenon would proliferate.

Rape Rings

The tone was set on May 8th, with the appearance of a double-ringed circle (95/01) in rape at Southease, a small village between Lewes and Newhaven. This was by far the earliest the phenomenon had ever visited the county, and at last Sussex had been treated to a rape formation with the crop in its gorgeous yellow prime. Not only was the arrival early for Sussex, it was only the second or third formation to appear anywhere in the country in 1995 and was the best. The very high and bushy rape stems had been laid down in bunches without any apparent damage or bruising to these brittle plants, with all the flower heads intact and the bushiness preserved. The swirl of the centre circle was magnificent, the stems curved in several different places to effect the spiral. Under a blue sky, walking through these bright circular pathways was a beautiful experience. Although it wasn't large, its quality and sheer charm made it a favourite amongst many researchers, many of whom travelled long distances to see their first formation of the year. The central circle was 24', the inner ring 47' by 6', and the outer ring 91' by 15'. About a hundred feet west up the field (the formation

Rings in rape at Southease, which appeared on 8th May (95/01), the earliest a formation has appeared in Sussex. Photo: Michael Hubbard.

was on quite a slope), its flat edge on a tramline, a perfect half grapeshot semicircle of 4' by 2' was found.

In 1995, CCCS Sussex carried out several extensive experiments with electrostatic meter devices to see if any electrical anomalies could be detected. Work had been briefly carried out in 1993. An electrostatic 'hotspot' was found on the north edge of the Southease central circle which consistently gave strange readings above the normal background static. Interestingly, at this very spot, a stem of rape was found which had been bent around at 90 degrees. Over the next few days, as the plant (which was taken for tests) dried out, the stem continued bending until it eventually completed one and a half loops!

Continuing the craving for attention the phenomenon seems to aspire to, the Southease rings, which bore a resemblance to the British RAF target symbol, appeared on the 50th Anniversary of VE day. That night, many people went up onto the downs of Firle Beacon to witness the commemorative bonfires lit that night. From there, many looked out across the River Ouse valley and saw the Southease formation looking back up at them from the hills opposite.

The Catherine Wheel

The next design to appear (95/02) was quite different, and arrived back at the old haunt of Alfriston, which had not seen any activity for several years. Many living in the region were pleased to see this area reactivated, as they didn't have to drive quite so far to get to these formations!

Quickly dubbed the 'Catherine wheel' by some, a quadruple-ringed circle in young barley, with four huge spiral arms (bearing a resemblance to the arms of 1994's 'galaxy' formations in Wiltshire) overlooked the road to Litlington and Lullington. This huge pattern appeared on May 31st in very immature crop and was not sharply defined from the ground as the laid crop was extremely bushy and barely flat at all. It was as if the crop had only been very lightly brushed down. It was not until seen from the air that its full glory and quite magnificent configuration was realised. The formation, which

Dusk falls over the vast 'Catherine wheel' at Alfriston (95/01). Photo: Steve Alexander

flowed anticlockwise (although the arms were seemingly spinning the other way), went from a tiny centre circle of 6', to an outside ring of a staggering 132'. The distance between the tip of one of the spiral arms to its counterpart opposite was 262'...

A number of interesting effects were observed within this formation: Where the tractor tramlines crossed the flattened parts, instead of being covered by the laid crop as usual, the circle-making force had left long standing curtains of crop marking the edges of the tramlines, so that wherever the tramlines were, one could see them as strips of unaffected crop which clearly had never been laid down with the rest of the floor pattern. Also, where the spiral arms emanated from the largest ring, some of the crop which had initially been swept into the flow of the arms had apparently decided it didn't want to go in that direction and so, bending several times at the nodes, reversed itself to flow neatly back into the lay of the large ring.

Several people reported strange effects on themselves and mechanical equipment whilst within this formation, a feature often reported in association with the phenomenon. Mobile telephone batteries were drained on one occasion while *Anglia Television* were filming inside for *The Magic and Mystery Show*, only to mysteriously refresh once outside, and there were reports of people experiencing extreme physical fatigue after only a short time within it. Some put this down to the strong earth energies which many believe are connected to the crop circles.

The pattern's location was also of interest. Sitting one and three quarter miles between the White Horse chalk carving which overlooks the Cuckmere valley to the south-west and the Long Man of Wilmington hill figure a mile to the east (which would itself be revisited at the end of the season), nearby local churches of historical interest seemed to play a part in its positioning. Drawing a line from Berwick church to Lullington church and another from Wilmington church to Alfriston church, the formation was situated exactly at the point where these two lines crossed. The wheel also made up one point of a two-dimensional representation of a tetrahedron which could be drawn by taking lines from it to the location of the 1994 Birling Gap shapes, Jevington church, and the subscriptions address of SC, the magazine produced by the Sussex group!

The Catherine wheel attracted a lot of attention, not least from another passing TV crew from *Meridian* ITV who decided it would make a good filler story for their evening news programme and stomped into it apparently without even asking the farmer, who was not best pleased with the formation's presence and the subsequent attention in the first place. He was probably even less pleased when *Meridian* broadcast the report that evening, giving the exact location to all and sundry across the south-east.

The Early Trigger

Why was Sussex treated to two such excellent events so early in the year, when the previous record had been the first week of June? The Sussex branch of the Centre for Crop Circle Studies started the pre-formation year with a huge burst of activity to mount the (humorously-titled) *Sussex Cerealogical Bonanza* weekend, the first ever crop circle conference staged in Sussex. This saw croppies from around the country gather at Burgess Hill for two days of circle-related information and entertainments, intended to start the season in style. Exactly one week after the *Bonanza* came the Southease rings, the beginning of one of Sussex's finest years yet for crop formations. Could it be that such a focusing of enthusiasm and energy from so many people in a new area for this type of gathering helped trigger the phenomenon into action locally?

1995

The Grass Grows Greener...

Alfriston was then visited again by the phenomenon - or something that appeared to be - on 23rd June, with a formation in uncultivated long grass (95/03) found on the hill facing the Catherine wheel, at Long Burgh, the old burial mound, now overgrown. Although very untidy, this, which was roughly circular, had all the details one might expect; bent nodes, flowed swirls, woven 'nests' rather like the effects observed at Birling Gap the previous year, and even what appeared to be a standing centre. The surrounding grass was about knee-high and there were no apparent trails into the flattened area which was 25' to the left of the South Downs Way footpath.

Curiously, drawing a line on a map between the Southease rings and the Alfriston Catherine wheel, the grass circle was directly on the same line. Long Burgh itself is reportedly the meeting place of many earth energy lines, and yet another burial mound, seemingly Neolithic, lies to the north of where the grass formation appeared.

A Meditational Success..?

Following on from the meditational experiments held in June 1993, some members of CCCS Sussex had continued their programme of attempting to interact with whatever was behind the circle-making force. In 1994, channelled information which came through the psychic Paul Bura at a meditation held on top of Cissbury Ring on a hot summer's day, had persuaded the group to take a different approach in 1995. Working on the assumption that perhaps patterns were already held within the memory of the earth energy grid before manifesting physically as crop circles, it was decided that the group should try and trigger such a pattern to appear in the fields themselves, rather like the exercise undertaken in 1993 where all the members concentrated on a certain shape, but this time using psychic guidance. The group gathered at sunset on the ancient site of Wolstonbury Hill, above Hurstpierpoint, on June 28th. Wolstonbury had, according to dowsers, been the energy sparking point for some of the formations which had previously appeared in the Pyecombe area. This year, nine people meditated on an earth energy line, using crystals and sound, in an effort to trigger a crop formation to appear at a chosen site a few miles away, near Devil's Dyke. Six musical notes were played during the meditation, as divined by Paul Bura. Barry Reynolds then interpreted these notes via the 'diatonic scale', a mathematical table which ultimately represents the white notes of a piano. Several researchers had already discovered a relationship between the numbers found in crop design dimensions to the diatonic scale. Barry predicted that if a formation were to appear in response to the experiment, the six notes could result in a pattern made up of six circular elements of differing size, which he drew on a piece of paper. The group did not expect a formation to instantly appear at the chosen site, but felt that if anything were to eventually appear there in subsequent months, or even years, it would have been a successful experiment.

Therefore, from this point of view, perhaps the most important formation of the year was the one which appeared at Felbridge, near East Grinstead on June 29th (95/04); a circle, above a larger ringed circle, which in turn was above a double ringed circle, etched into long-eared wheat. *Six circular elements of differing sizes.* This appeared on the very night of the Wolstonbury experiment - and only a few hundred feet from the location of the 'monocycle' (93/08) in the same field two years previously. The only strangeness was the site - more than several miles away from the chosen place where it was 'expected'. Why had the shape appeared here and what was the connection? The answer could be found by drawing a line on a map between Wolstonbury, the site

72

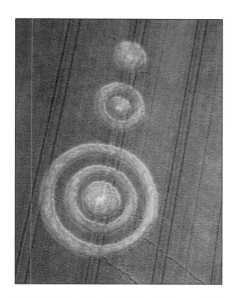

The Felbridge rings (95/04) which seemingly appeared in response to the meditational experiment carried out on Wolstonbury Hill. Photo: Michael Hubbard

The finesse with which many crop circles are laid was demonstrated excellently in the Felbridge formation. Note how the outer edge of the large ring shown here takes just some of the stems from a single seed hole into the flow (some from **behind** standing stems!), leaving others untouched. Photo: Andy Thomas

The Felbridge rings (95/04) were completely secluded and virtually invisible from the ground until right next to the formation. Photo: Andy Thomas.

selected near Devil's Dyke, and Felbridge - the alignment line went very close to the field which contained the formation. Independent dowsers then discovered that the *energy* line which connected the original site to Wolstonbury, continued on EXACTLY through the centre of the Felbridge rings. It seems the CCCS Sussex interaction experiments finally had a positive result. Perhaps not quite the result expected, as the meditational energy had inexplicably gone in the opposite direction intended, but one encouraging enough to call a success.

What of the formation itself? The farmer alerted CCCS Sussex to its presence - a welcome exception! Like its predecessor in the same secluded field, it could not be seen from anywhere but above (which it probably was - Felbridge lies directly under a flightpath out of Gatwick airport) and was invisible until standing at the edge of the crop itself on the mown grass strip which bordered the sown part of the field. This grass strip, and the hospitality of the farmer, meant that researchers had the novelty of being able to drive directly up to the formation, which lay only about 50' in from the edge. Many photographs were taken by standing on car rooftops... The solace and seclusion offered by this quiet location meant that CCCS Sussex was able to carry out several experiments and activities without disturbance or calling attention to itself. We were even allowed to have a 'open day' for many who had never witnessed a circle for themselves - on condition that everyone took samples of grain, to be grown on in seasonal generations in the US as part of an experiment to see whether crop laid down in formations is genetically affected.

The pattern was very crisp and well-formed, as if a giant pastry-cutter had stamped itself on the field. A demonstration of the finesse and accuracy with which this was created was apparent at the edge of the largest ring, where individual stalks had been pulled into the flow of the arc from seed-holes which had unaffected crop still standing (several stems appear to grow from one source but they are in fact individual plants sown together). In some cases, these individual stems were pulled into the ring from *behind* standing stalks - which demonstrates neatly why many crop formations cannot simply be stomped out with planks of wood.

The design was aligned directly on top of the tractor tramlines (rather like the first national pictograms of 1990) which ran exactly east-west in this part of the field. Curiously, a hundred feet in either direction from the formation, the tramlines kinked abruptly to take another orientation - it lay perfectly between these two kinks. Some geometric ratio correlations were also found; for instance, the single circle diameter was exactly that of the ring from the ringed circle, which in turn was the same diameter as the inner ring of the double-ringed circle. All crop was laid clockwise. The single circle was 18', the ringed circle 29' and the double-ringed circle 67'.

One girl who took part in the CCCS Sussex 'open day' claimed she was cured of a bad throat infection after spending some time in the formation. There are accounts of 'healings' having taken place in other circles across the country, but also stories of illness having been caused, although whether this is due to unusual 'energies' emanating from the shapes or can be related to pesticides in the crop isn't known.

ADAS (Agricultural Development and Advisory Service), a division of the Ministry of Agriculture, performed some tests on soil samples from a number of crop formations in 1995, one of which (another being the Alfriston wheel) was the Felbridge pictogram. The results showed a significantly higher amount of nitrates in the soil below the pattern compared to control samples outside. Unfortunately, before any further work could be carried out, the department of ADAS carrying out the tests was suddenly shut down in mysterious circumstances.

Two Oddities And A Smiley Face

In 1994, the area just above Chichester was visited by some lovely formations such as the ones at East Dean. In 1995 the area wasn't completely neglected, but seemed to have an 'experimental' feel to it instead.

At Kingley Vale forest, near Stoughton, a small design was found in soil and pine needles on 22nd June (95/05). Kingley Vale is, historically, one of the last remaining groves of the most ancient Yew Forest in Europe, and is considered a magic and meaningful place by many. In a glade between a triangle of three large Yews, a symbol was discovered on the ground. Small sticks were aligned in a radial configuration from a tiny circle at the centre, surrounded by three rings made up from mounds of forest floor materials. Ten 'J' shapes emanated outwards from the outer ring. Fallen pine needles were swirled in just the way one would expect with crop and no footprints around it were visible, even though the soil was very dry and dusty.

The formation was only about 4' across and was found by CCCS Sussex member Judith Newman while out walking with her brother one hot afternoon. She swears that they had already walked into the same glade only ten minutes before and nothing was there. When they returned, the symbol had appeared. They had seen no-one else in that part of the woods and the shape was so finely constructed that it was impossible to see, despite its modest size, how anyone could have created such a complex pattern so quickly. The next day, Judith returned to take some photographs, only to have her camera jam as soon as she tried to use it. The camera had never played up previously.

This was certainly a very unusual formation, which some have speculated may have been in some way connected to sun symbols used in ancient earth magic rituals, as it was the summer solstice the day it appeared. Others have pointed out its resemblance to a symbol used by the African Dogon tribe to represent the 'descent of the Nommos' from the stars. The Dogons believe their race originated from people known as 'the Nommos' from a planet in the star system Sirius. (Interestingly, the Dogons have held detailed knowledge of certain stars and planets for centuries, which modern astronomy is only now discovering for itself.)

Further east, towards Arundel, at Binsted, another strange formation occurred (95/06), this time in connection with a sighting of lights the night it arrived - another instance was to occur before the year was out. Helen Whitlock, on whose land it appeared, witnessed a bright cigar-shaped object in the sky at about three in the morning on 1st July, as she was out walking her dogs (a light sleeper!). The object was about 7' long and seemed to have a physical dimension to it. As it hovered about 50' high over her farmstead, a "band of mist" circled around its middle and either side of the long edges of the cigar were four lines of light, the inner two bright red and the outer ones metallic green. After a few minutes, the object slowly moved down towards the end of the garden before abruptly winking out.

Two mornings later, in a fenced off area of rushes and undergrowth around a large pond, her husband Robin was shocked to find a large patch (about 20' by 15') of flattened water rushes at the foot of a steep bank, in no describable shape. This was directly below where the peculiar object had previously vanished. There were no traces of anyone having broken into the area, which was surrounded by barbed wire, and there was no apparent physical damage to the plants. Although the shape of the 'splurge' was fairly indiscernible, the rushes appeared to be laid and swirled in much the same way one would expect in a more usual event. To anyone's knowledge, this was the first instance in England of a formation having been reported in rushes, made even more intriguing by the apparent connection with the strange cigar-shaped object.

Somehow, without the witnesses having even spoken to the press, this story made it into the local newspapers, with all the inaccuracies one might expect, 'quoting' Mrs Whitlock as saying that perhaps she had "one Pimms too many" that night. A fine example of ethical journalism! Interestingly, the nearest neighbour in this remote village of Binsted was Jenni Cassel, who alerted us to the story - the same lady who had been painting East Dean by night when the events occurred there the year before.

There were another three formations in this area, which attracted little attention; two circles, one large with a long emanating pathway, the other much smaller, were discovered in wheat at Compton, near Chichester (95/13), but weren't reported until after harvest. The more dubious word 'MONO' was spotted laid in a field just inside Sussex, east of Petersfield. Another dubious configuration of thin rings and semi-circles (95/11) was found in wheat at Cocking, near Midhurst on 16th July, near some children's playing fields. After initial excitement, when aerial shots revealed it to be a winking smiley-face smoking a cigarette, enthusiasm for it waned somewhat, although those who entered it said the main ring of the 'face' was fairly well laid, giving rise to the possibility that the original ring was 'genuine' and that the eyes and mouth were added later by local 'artists'..! Most, though, were understandably sceptical.

More scepticism dogged a formation which appeared in wheat at Saltdean on 2nd July (95/07) for the same reasons. Saltdean is a large estate which sits in the valley between Rottingdean and Peacehaven, and crop fields surround it on the downs overlooking the area. The formation was on the east side of the downs above a sharp grassy cliff. The best view to be had was by ascending the steep road of the west side of Saltdean and looking back across the valley, which revealed a ringed single circle with a long path below it and some kind of lettering to the right.

Closer inspection revealed the pattern to be a neat single circle of about 30', flowed anticlockwise, which appeared to have had several crude additions put on to it afterwards. The path below, which split off into three, looked like some kind of attempt to turn the circle into the head of a stick figure. The ring had also apparently been added, and the unidentified word turned out to be a rather indelicate swear word. Aerial photography helped clarify this! All these additions were very roughly constructed and the lay was extremely messy bearing no relation to the quality of the actual circle itself, which was neatly spiralled. There seems more of a serious case here (in the absence of any hard information) that the single circle was 'genuine' and local youths, spotting it from the estate, went up and added their own 'artwork' later.

Seven Different Crops

By now, one thing had become noticeable about the 1995 Sussex season - the great variety of the plants which all the formations had appeared in so far. Each time it had been something different: oilseed rape, barley, long grass, long-eared wheat, forest floor materials, water rushes and finally, good old basic wheat. Never before had quite such a diversity in succession been noted. Quite what was to be read into this wasn't clear, but perhaps it was intended as a series of lessons for people to acquaint themselves with the many different effects that could be had by the circle-making force working with different mediums. Overall, once again, it was a reminder that with the crop circle phenomenon, all that should be expected is the unexpected.

Lights Over Denton, Circles Below

In the summer months, the Newhaven area became, briefly, a hotspot for UFO sightings. These stories were so numerous that they made it into the local press. Many people, including town councillor Gill Dawson, witnessed a large bright light or metallic shape moving purposefully around the sky. Quoted in the *Sussex Express*, Mrs Dawson, who viewed the light through binoculars, described it as a "large, flat, hexagonal object". As far as crop formations were concerned, the Southease rings had opened up this coastal area early in the year for paranormal phenomena, and Alfriston was not so very far away. Was the reactivation of this area in some way connected to the sightings of the light? Directly below where many of the major sightings had been made, a large formation appeared (95/08) on 9th July as if to cement the connection, just outside Newhaven, at Denton Corner, overlooking the A259 coastal road to Seaford.

Basically a large dumbbell in wheat, from the smaller top circle a long path emanated at a 45 degree angle, leading to a perfect semi-circle with two centres in the crop lay. The swirls and layering in this formation were impressive. The path leading to the

The formation at Denton, Newhaven (95/08). Photo: Michael Hubbard.

semi-circle even changed its direction two-thirds up, with a swirled centre as its junction point. A thin ring orbited the largest of the dumbbell's circles, although its quality was less good. A number of small pathways from the main parts appeared later, although only an arc which almost linked the two shafts seemed to share the same qualities as the original. The large dumbbell circle was 72', the pathway from it 30' by 6', the small circle 32', the long pathway from it 65' by 4', and the semicircle's flat edge was 42'. All the crop was laid clockwise.

This pattern was extremely visible from the busy road and was probably seen by more people than any other Sussex formation in 1995, although its exact shape couldn't be discerned from that angle. Certainly, barely a hour seemed to go by without someone pulling over and hopping into the field to view this wondrous arrival. Entirely without permission of course, but it does illustrate the pulling power of this incredible phenomenon. Despite all the scepticism in the media and all the disinformation about crop circles, the public's curiosity remains, unconvinced that there isn't something very strange and special going on.

Denton is close to the busy ferry port which links Newhaven to Dieppe in France. Was it coincidence that the long shaft with the semi-circle, which bore a passing resemblance to a nuclear mushroom cloud, pointed directly at our neighbours across the Channel, bearing in mind that the formation appeared the month the French announced they would be recommencing nuclear weapons testing in the South Pacific?

The Live Exports Mystery

The more traditional area for Sussex circle activity wasn't deserted in 1995; in the same field and almost the same spot as the 'insectogram' or snail formation at Mill Hill, Shoreham, in 1993, a similar looking design to its predecessor appeared in wheat around 8th July (95/09) in the form of a dumbbell, ringed at one end, with standing centres, a separate triangle (also with a standing centre), and a rather charming 'cloverleaf' shape with three standing crescents. The cloverleaf in particular was very complex in its construction. Like 1993, the dumbbell had two uneven-lengthed 'boxes' either side of the connecting shaft and the nearby triangle was placed at almost exactly the same angle to the main formation in both cases. The circle-making force clearly has a good sense of continuity.

The overall length of the dumbbell was 110', the large ringed circle (including the ring) 54', the small circle 27', the triangle an average of 33' each side, and the cloverleaf the same. Looking deceptively small from a distance, this didn't stop local children from spilling easily into the shapes from the nearby footpath and the once clear edges were much worn down by harvest time. The patterns lay almost at the lowest point of the two slopes which make up the field and thus could not be seen from the A27, despite its close proximity.

A very strange 'coincidence' - a word synonymous with crop circles by now - was noted immediately, which would take on even more significance a few days later. Shoreham, another important Sussex port, was at the centre of a storm this summer when public outcries over the exportation of live veal calves spilled over into sometimes violent protests across the country. As one of the major port facilities for the trade, local feeling ran high in Shoreham. Although rather old when discovered, the crop formations appeared at Mill Hill much later than the words 'BAN LIVE EXPORTS' (or something obviously intended to read as that) which had already been crudely burned into the crop with chemicals by protesters several weeks before in the same field. Perhaps something had drawn the circle-making force to place its artistry next to these words. It was almost the reverse situation to the Saltdean scenario, where a circle had appeared and humans had added their own graffiti. Here, the crop circles had added their presence to graffiti already there. The following development threw this event into a more significant light.

On 23rd July, a similarly designed but much larger pictogram appeared in wheat at Upper Beeding a few miles away (95/12). This time the triangle was missing but the cloverleaf shape, now with full standing rings instead of crescents, had attached itself to the bottom of the dumbbell instead of being a separate component.

And in the same field, again the words 'BAN LIVE EXPORTS' had already been crudely placed there with chemicals several weeks previously. There was no doubt that the creators of the crop formations were not those of the writing, which was very poorly

These shapes at Shoreham (95/09) appeared directly adjacent to a live exports protest slogan daubed onto the crop with chemicals but were clearly not of the same authorship. Photo: Michael Hubbard.

executed in both cases. Something about the placing of these words had subsequently attracted the crop formations on both occasions. Was the circle-making force adding its support to the protest or, as some have considered, were the shapes placed there to balance the negative energies (however well-intentioned) which the protesters may have been giving out when spraying their chemicals onto the crop to create the lettering?

The formation was very well laid and clear-cut and due to its size could be seen for miles around, especially as one descended the Bostal Road down into Steyning. The outer ring was 95', the small circle 35', the boxes 4' by 13', and the overall length an impressive 213'. Some of the standing rings of the cloverleaf had been eclipsed by the flattened rings, the lay of the crop suggesting that the three rings must have been laid down simultaneously, not one after the other.

This was the first formation in Sussex to have a definite and unambiguous connection with peculiar aerial lights, courtesy of a man who lived opposite the field. Glancing out of his window at about two o'clock the night the pictogram appeared, he was amazed to see several small multi-coloured lights weaving about in the field. After a few minutes, the lights moved swiftly up into the sky and out of sight. It would seem he was witness to the creation of this design, with the attendant light phenomena which has been reported so often before in other parts of the country, although this differed from the Binsted incident in that no discernible *object* was detected. After much local press attention to the story, which somehow became public knowledge, this eyewitness subsequently retracted his remarks, saying that he saw nothing, perhaps over fears of losing his privacy. CCCS Sussex, who were the first to speak with him, were happy that his original story was true, especially as they tallied with so many similar reports elsewhere.

The direction in which the formation seemed to point was across the Adur valley, directly towards perhaps the most spectacular Sussex event of 1995.

1995

The Time Tunnel

Resembling in many ways the 'time tunnel' device from the old television series of the same name, a set of six incredible off-centre rings appeared in wheat at the foot of Cissbury Ring, at Lychpole Bottom behind Sompting, on 15th July (95/10). At last, the site which seemed to have been at the heart of so much of the crop circle activity, not to mention CCCS Sussex experiments, had been graced with a formation of its own. Viewed from above, the design had a startling hypnotic effect, and was an exhilarating sight. The precision with which this must have been executed, especially given the boldness of its off-centre geometry, was mind-boggling and the view from the nearby Bostal Road was magnificent, causing many motorists to pull over onto the verge at all times of the day.

Inside the formation, its size was even more impressive, although the quality of the actual crop was poor across the whole field, and surprisingly low for the time of year. It was on a deceptively steep slope, which made for good viewing from the road but also made it a tiring process walking around it! The rings averaged a width of 10ft, ranging from 15' at their widest to 5' at the thinnest. The total diameter was 238'!

The Cissbury Ring formations (95/10) in their final configuration, the largest complex of shapes to date in Sussex. Photo: Andy Thomas.

As if its already massive size wasn't enough, three new huge patterns then appeared alongside it in the same field, on 25th July; a triangle, a large circle and an elaborate dumbbell of rings, a three-circled celtic cross and spokes made up of sixteen separate rectangular boxes. These boxes were linked by an incredibly thin ring of about one stem's width. From the road, the sight of a field almost entirely covered by formations was quite amazing. The new dumbbell length was 248', the triangle about 30' each side and the single circle 120'. However, from the air, it was apparent that the additions weren't nearly as precise as the original rings, although they remained impressive nonetheless. This led to the inevitable conclusion from some - who had not entered them - that the additions were man-made. Those who examined them in detail felt differently, so complex was the construction, and from the ground it could be seen that the imperfections occurred where the dumbbell ring crossed the tramlines and at its lowest and highest points on the steep slope. The discrepancies in its shape may then be attributable to what is known as 'gap-seeking', a phenomenon occasionally noted before with crop circles, where the circle-making force seems to momentarily divert into any sizeable gap in the standing crop, before correcting itself.

Laying under and at times *over* the flattened crop of the additional dumbbell and circle were thin paths which seemed to have trickled down from the original rings, almost as if energy from the first formation had suddenly run through the crop and triggered a whole series of new events further away. Astonishingly, the location of the new dumbbell was precisely on top of where CCCS Sussex had taken control samples when collecting stems for laboratory testing the evening before the additions appeared. For the first time ever, we had samples from the same position in a field before and after a formation was created. Did the very act of taking the control samples in this case reactivate that part of the field to create new shapes?

Police Stories

Jason Porthouse had a disturbing run-in with the police while in this formation, despite having entry permission from the landowner. Because of the introduction of the government's Criminal Justice Act in 1995 which made trespass a criminal offence, not a civil one, the police were far more vigilant about people entering farmer's fields. Farmers in Hampshire even offered a £1000 reward for any information leading to the apprehension of 'those responsible' for making the crop designs damaging their land (when an invisible circle-making energy takes the dock in court, it could be rather interesting). Earlier in the year, some researchers had minor run-ins with the police at both Alfriston and Upper Beeding, where at the latter, due to a misunderstanding with the farmer, the CCCS Sussex team even found their vehicles blocked in by cars to prevent them leaving the area before questioning!

Jason found himself almost face-to-face with the local police helicopter, based at nearby Shoreham airport, while at Cissbury. The helicopter, in a rather dangerous manoeuvre, came in very close to hover literally feet above the rings, taking photographs of the formation - and Jason and his friends, who were still inside. Although buffeted by the downdraft of the helicopter blades, they stood their ground. At one point the helicopter flew over to the area where the cars were parked, presumably taking note of registration numbers, before flying back, even lower. Eventually it moved on its way. This was fairly typical of other reports of helicopter harassment which had occurred in Wiltshire, but those craft were usually military. For a police helicopter to act in this way was unusual.

There is a wry coda to the story: Perturbed by the incident, Jason decided to telephone the police to find out what the helicopter business was about. Surprisingly, he actually managed to track down one of the pilots of the helicopter to speak to. The officer was inevitably cagey but warmed after a while. He then began to tell Jason of UFOs they had seen from the police helicopter in their time - and asked whether we knew about the mass sightings of strange lights which had been seen over Bognor Regis earlier in the summer... an unexpected exchange of police information!

To everyone's surprise, with August still to come, there would be only one more formation discovered after the Cissbury events...

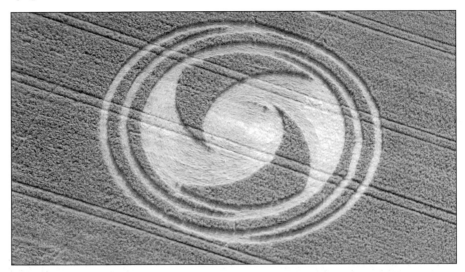

The 1995 Wilmington formation (95/14) looks simple. In fact, this is a very difficult formation to make a scale drawing of, so complex is its design – yet another reminder of the incredibly sophisticated level the crop circle phenomenon operates on. Photo: Michael Hubbard.

Gazing out across the gorgeous Sussex landscape from inside the Wilmington formation (95/14). Photo: Andy Thomas.

EPILOGUE:
THE LAST WORD FROM THE LONG MAN

The last formation to appear in Sussex in 1995 (95/14), and indeed to date at the time of writing, was a circular pattern of interlocking standing crescents and two 'angel fish'-type designs on a flattened bed of crop at Wilmington, directly to the right of the famous Long Man chalk carving and just over the hill from the Alfriston Catherine wheel. It appeared in wheat on the same night as the later Cissbury shapes, 25th July, but as a formation in its own right rather than an addition, it was treated as the last glyph of the year. The two landscape markings looked somehow comfortable together as they gazed down at the visitors' car park, confirming once again that just as important to the circle-

The Long Man of Wilmington with his new, if temporary, companion (95/14) etched into the field beside him. Photo: Andy Thomas.

making force is *where* the design is placed in the landscape, not just the look of the design itself. Many who came to see the hill figure were unexpectedly treated to their first sight of a crop circle.

The accuracy with which the pattern had been executed was again quite breathtaking. At first glance it looked deceptively simple but this turned out to be the most difficult Sussex formation yet to make a diagram of. The two very fine crescents were interlocked with each other with such finesse that the mind ached to think how this might have been achieved. The points of the crescents were so thin that they culminated in a curtain of single standing stems. The central swirl of the floor lay was a very tight 'S' shape, which flowed around the two curving arrows of the 'angel fish', bearing a faint resemblance to the classic yin/yang symbol. The formation was 148' across.

The view from it was stunning, looking out across a patchwork of fields being rapidly harvested as the season's yield came to a premature end, farmers racing to get the crop in before the scorching heat of one of the warmest summers of the decade could wither it. Usually researchers could expect at least another month of circle-hunting, but with so few fields left standing at the beginning of August, the likelihood of another formation rapidly lessened. No-one in Sussex guessed at the time that the Wilmington event would be the last of the year.

As ever, when crop circles are present, the conversations sparked amongst the sightseers in the tourist car-park, looking up in wonder at the almost galaxy-shaped imprint on the hill, were fascinating to behold, as they discussed the possibility of life elsewhere and what the pattern might mean. Even the sceptical among them couldn't help but show a little awe. Surely the very purpose of the formations is to inspire such conversation and speculation?

Oddly, however, although the Long Man stood directly to the left of the design, standing in the crop pattern itself the most that could be seen of the ancient chalk figure was his head, just peering over the brow of the hill on which the field lay. Somehow, there seemed to be a metaphor for the entire phenomenon in this curious image.

The Long Man, like the crop formations, is an enigma, visually stunning and full of ancient symbolism. He stares out across the landscape for all to see and yet his true origins are a mystery. No-one really knows who made him, or why. And yet thousands are drawn to view this wonder every year, unaware, apart from basic historical interest, of what really motivates their pull towards this symbol, nor what it means. They only know that something about the Long Man makes artistic sense in a way that can't be articulated on an intellectual level. So it is with the crop circles. They remain a mystery, despite all the speculation, both sceptical and metaphysical. But their striking beauty and mathematical qualities elevate them to a level that needs only to be understood with the heart, not the thinking mind.

Whatever their origins and true purpose, the circles have instigated in many a yearning to question the world around them, and, ultimately, existence itself. The enquiries they inspire over how they might have been constructed and what the symbolism means, finally give way to asking *why* they are appearing. Who or what is creating them? Where does this force come from and what is its nature? Most importantly, what is it trying to tell us, if there is a message at all? This then opens the gates to a whole new way of thinking which threatens the conventional world-view of Newtonian predictability in favour of a universe where what amounts to magic really does happen all around us.

Even if, against all the evidence, an assumption were made for a moment that the crop formations were simply the work of human landscape artists, the questions would be only a little less profound. How could they create them so accurately? Why would they feel compelled to manifest these symbols? What would it tell us about the collective subconscious that it could throw up the blueprints for these deeply divined mandalas - what significance would they have for the human condition? Even if this unlikely scenario is considered, a mystery still remains.

The Long Man peering over the brow of the hill at the elaborate design in the field nearby may represent us as a civilisation. Miraculous events are happening all around us, in this case in the fields, there for us to see - if we make the effort to look beyond the narrow confines of our own daily lives. They are there in front of our eyes but we must look up from other concentrations to notice them. The crop circles don't impose themselves on our lives, we have a choice. We must go to them if we wish to receive whatever wisdom we may, whether transmitted from outside through the symbols, or simply divined by our own minds from inner contemplation. Many people have peered over their hills and noticed the wonders around them, and now actively seek to learn more.

Where the phenomenon will go from here remains unknowable; it has always shown a resistance to predictability. If, as many have speculated, the formations are a portent, a signal - or warning - of important times ahead, perhaps when these times arrive the patterns will have done their work and they will appear no more. In the period until then, maybe the phenomenon will continue to evolve and develop, surprising us at every turn with the size, designs and geographical distribution of the crop formations. Whether Sussex will continue to play a part in this development no-one can say, but a legacy has been left here, through memories and records of the times the circles were among us, that cannot be taken away. This book has been compiled with a view to helping record that legacy for later generations, however many, or few, wish to delve into it from the unknown future.

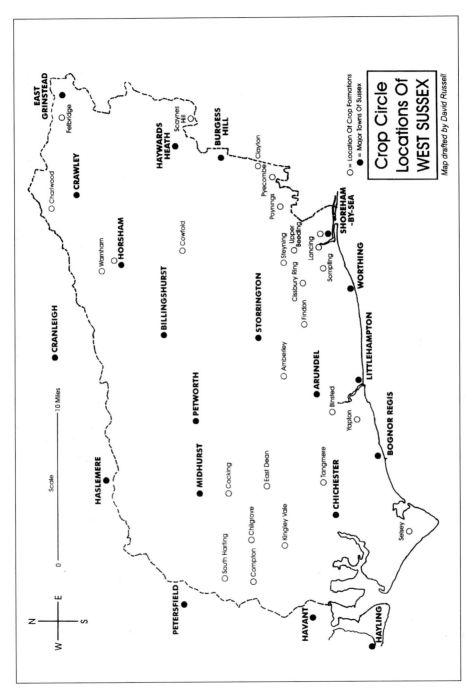

Crop Circle
Locations Of
WEST SUSSEX

O = Location Of Crop Formations
● = Major Towns Of Sussex

Map drafted by David Russell

N
W — E
S

Scale

0 ———— 10 Miles

EAST GRINSTEAD
Felbridge
Charlwood
CRAWLEY
HAYWARDS HEATH
Scaynes Hill
BURGESS HILL
Clayton
Pyecombe
Poynings
HORSHAM
Warnham
Cowfold
BILLINGSHURST
CRANLEIGH
STORRINGTON
Steyning
Upper Beeding
Cissbury Ring
Lancing
Sompting
SHOREHAM-BY-SEA
WORTHING
Findon
Amberley
ARUNDEL
LITTLEHAMPTON
PETWORTH
Binsted
Yapton
BOGNOR REGIS
HASLEMERE
MIDHURST
Cocking
East Dean
Tangmere
CHICHESTER
South Harting
Compton
Chilgrove
Kingley Vale
Selsey
PETERSFIELD
HAVANT
HAYLING

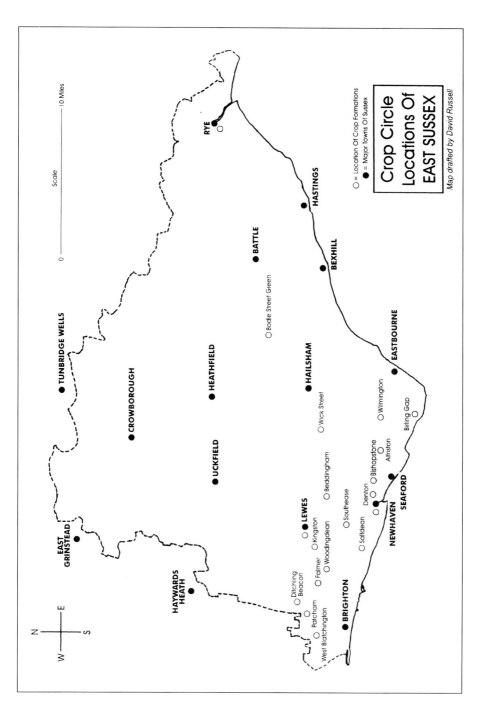

Crop Circle
Locations Of
EAST SUSSEX

O = Location Of Crop Formations
● = Major Towns Of Sussex

Map drafted by David Russell

87

APPENDIX 1

THE CENTRE FOR CROP CIRCLE STUDIES, SUSSEX BRANCH

The Centre For Crop Circle Studies (CCCS) was founded in 1990 and is an international organisation dedicated to investigating, recording and disseminating information on the crop circle phenomenon. The English section of the organisation is made up from many regional branches across the country, of which Sussex is the largest in membership numbers. The Sussex group was founded in 1991 and is one of the most active branches, researching the appearance of crop formations in East and West Sussex. It meets once a month, usually on the third alternating Tuesday or Thursday of the month, at the following venue:

The Scout Centre
Station Road
Burgess Hill
West Sussex

The entrance to the Scout Centre can be found just opposite the Potters Arms public house. Meetings are held in the upper room, begin at 8.00pm and are usually a lively mixture of the latest news from the world's crop fields in a friendly atmosphere of animated discussion. Guest speakers from the world of cerealogy and beyond regularly give presentations at branch meetings, especially in the winter months. A nominal attendance fee of £1.00 is charged, except for guest speaker evenings, which are charged at £2.00.

For further details about the branch and local meetings, contact the address below:

CCCS Sussex
44 Meadow Lane
Burgess Hill
West Sussex
RH15 9JA

Tel: 01444 232873

Details correct at time of going to press.

APPENDIX 2

SC - THE MONTHLY JOURNAL OF CROP CIRCLES AND BEYOND

Andy Thomas is editor of this publication, which has the largest annualised readership figures of any crop circle journal in the world. SC - which once stood for *Sussex Circular* - began life as the newsletter for CCCS Sussex but quickly expanded to become one of the most respected and enjoyable sources of general circle information. A monthly A5 booklet, it now has readers across the globe and covers national and international events while retaining its extensive coverage of crop formations which appear in Sussex. SC's lively style has attracted many accolades with its up-to-the-minute news, reviews, reports and features on all the significant happenings in the circles world.

Subscription to SC is currently £10.00 per year (UK), £13.00 (Europe) and £18.00 (US & overseas). Individual copies are £1.00. Currency for cheques and POs sent from abroad must be made out in Sterling, drawn on a bank with a British branch. If you would like to subscribe to SC, please send a cheque, payable to **SCR**, to the following address:

**SC
36 Graham Crescent
Mile Oak
Portslade
East Sussex
BN41 2YB**

Tel: 01273 885117

If you wish to contact Andy Thomas, please write to this address:

**Andy Thomas
c/o 10 Winterbourne Close
Lewes
East Sussex
BN7 1JY**

Tel: 01273 474711

APPENDIX 3

CIRCULAR SUSSEX: THE SUSSEX CROP CIRCLE VIDEO

A video cassette documentary by Andy Thomas entitled *Circular Sussex: Crop Circles in Sussex* is available, showing actual footage of some of the crop formations covered in this book.

In 1993 and 1994, Andy Thomas recorded many formations in detail and the work of the Centre for Crop Circle Studies surveying team. *Circular Sussex*, a half-hour programme professionally edited and presented, documents the appearance of the crop circle phenomenon in Sussex with music by Andy Thomas and David Swingland and narration by Paul Bura.

The video is available on PAL VHS cassette (English standard system) and costs £8.95 (including p&p).

To order a copy, please send a cheque/PO payable to A S THOMAS, to the address below. Currency for cheques and POs sent from abroad must be made out in Sterling, drawn on a bank with a British branch.

Circular Sussex
c/o 10 Winterbourne Close
Lewes
East Sussex
BN7 1JY

APPENDIX 4

RECOMMENDED READING

A number of books about the crop circle phenomenon have become standard reference reading, which some readers may like to seek out. The best of these are listed below, with brief comments by myself. Not all of the following are necessarily still in print but copies can often be found at circle-related events or from specialist collectors outlets.

CIRCULAR EVIDENCE (Bloomsbury, London, 1989) by Pat Delgado and Colin Andrews. The essential guide to the early years of the phenomenon in England.

THE CROP CIRCLE ENIGMA (Gateway Books, Bath, 1990) edited by Ralph Noyes. An across-the-board selection of essays on the origins of the phenomenon with a variety of views expressed in a well-presented format.

CROP CIRCLES: HARBINGERS OF WORLD CHANGE (Gateway Books, Bath 1991) edited by Alick Bartholomew. Follow up to *The Crop Circle Enigma*, in the same format, this time concentrating on the meaning of the phenomenon rather than the mechanics.

THE CIRCLES EFFECT AND ITS MYSTERIES (Artetech, Bradford-on-Avon, 1989) by George Terence Meaden. The weather vortex theory still seemed plausible when this was published but this dated volume still has some valid ideas on the mechanics of circle-making and some good records of early formations.

CIPHERS IN THE CROPS (Gateway Books, Bath, 1992) edited by Beth Davis. An excellent little book of essays, concentrating on the origins and meanings of three important formations from 1991; the Barbury Castle triangle, the Mandelbrot Set and the Froxfield 'serpent'.

THE COSMIC CONNECTION (Gateway Books, Bath, 1995) by Michael Hesemann. Updated English version of a German book released in 1993, proposing ETs and flying saucers as the answer to the crop circles. Even if this opinion isn't shared it gives a good overview of the phenomenon with some stunning photos.

DOWSING THE CROP CIRCLES (Gothic Image, Glastonbury, 1991) edited by John Michell. Slim but informative booklet of essays compiled from *The Cerealogist* magazine, examining the art of dowsing earth energies in relation to the circles. Includes a chapter by David Tilt with references to Sussex formations.

APPENDIX 5

HOW TO REPORT A CROP FORMATION

CCCS Sussex relies on the eyes and ears of everyone to help discover new crop formations. If you see a crop formation in Sussex that you think may not have been reported, please follow the procedure below:

1) Do not, if you can avoid the temptation, enter the crop formation, and certainly not without permission from the landowner. The ideal research environment is when formations are in pristine condition. Even one person walking inside a formation can destroy valuable evidence CCCS may need to see. Don't harrass the farmers as their co-operation is vital for further research. CCCS Sussex are already in contact with many of the farmers in the Sussex area.

2) Telephone CCCS Sussex on **01273 474711.** If there is no reply, telephone **01444 232873.** You should then be able to find out whether or not CCCS Sussex are already aware of the formation. If no-one is available, answerphones are normally in operation, so leave a message at the least, giving the following information:

i)   Location, as detailed as possible
ii) The formation's shape, the crop it is in etc.
iii) Your name and contact number

News of the latest formations which have appeared feature regularly each month in SC.

THE AUTHOR

Andy Thomas was born and bred in Lewes, East Sussex, where he lives today with his wife and son.

A musician, composer, and writer by profession, Andy edited and published Paul Bura's book *Joeb - Servant of Gaia* and is the resident film reviewer for *Steppin' Out* magazine.

Andy is editor of the monthly crop circle magazine SC, which has a world-wide readership, and is a founder member of the Centre for Crop Circle Studies, Sussex branch. He regularly lectures around England on crop circles and paranormal phenomena.

Andy Thomas

INDEX

The two formations at East Dean, 1994, seen together (94/07 and 94/08). Photo: Steve Alexander.

S. B. Publications publish a wide range of local interest titles on Sussex and other counties. For details write (enclosing S.A.E.) to:
S. B. Publications, c/o 19 Grove Road, Seaford, East Sussex BN25 1TP